Anticipatory Management

10 Power Tools for Achieving Excellence into the 21st Century

Anticipatory Management

10 Power Tools for Achieving Excellence into the 21st Century

by

William C. Ashley
Ashley & Associates

James L. Morrison
University of North Carolina
at Chapel Hill

Leesburg, Virginia

Issue Action Publications, Inc.
207 Loudoun Street, S.E.
Leesburg, Virginia 22075
Telephone (703) 777-8450
Facsimile (703) 777-8484

Library of Congress Catalog Card Number: 95-080645

ISBN 0-913869-05-8
First printing: November 1995
Printed in the United States of America

Preface: Bringing the Tools and Techniques of Anticipation to Management

The difficulty in times of turbulence is not the turbulence, but to respond with yesterday's logic.

— Peter Drucker

Given that change is inevitable, the real issue for managers is whether that change will happen belatedly, in a crisis atmosphere, or with foresight, in a calm and considered manner; whether the transformation agenda will be set by a company's more prescient competitors or by its own point of view. . .

— Hamel and Prahalad, (1994)

The culture of most organizations over the last 40 years was to grow bigger. The focus has been on increasing work force productivity, using resources more effectively, and obtaining more yield from investments — in other words, maximizing the bottom line.

To achieve these ends, the paradigm was to do more, do better, do longer, do faster, do harder, do bigger. If a statue were to be erected to the achievements of business over the last four decades, that statement would make a fitting inscription. The monument itself would be a sleek automobile with windshield and headlights covered and only the rearview mirror and the side windows for vision. Why? American businesses have characteristically limited their perspectives to either looking back at how things were done in the past and/or laterally to see how competition is or is not doing something. These practices cannot continue if U.S. businesses expect to survive the coming global shakeout.

Transcending the status quo and looking ahead

to the future requires new sets of managerial skills. Unfortunately, managers increasingly are being asked to prop up outdated paradigms in terms of weak products, services, and processes in the face of social, technological, economic, environmental, and political change that often makes obsolete what the organization currently is protecting. Hindsightedness and rigidity hinders managers from discarding old methodologies and embracing the new ones, an intransigence supported by pithy homilies such as:

- We are the competition; no one can touch us.
- Entry into our business will endanger the soundness and safety of the industry.
- Actions like that will lead to the loss of many valuable jobs in the industry.
- Our market is so well covered by us, no one else could possibly get in.
- Our customers are dedicated to us; they would never leave us.
- Our equipment, technology, products, services and processes are state-of-the-art.
- With all the money we put into training, TQM, MBO, and R&D, we are head and shoulders ahead of the competition.

The affliction of hindsightedness affects all organizations, but it is particularly pernicious among firms with successful products and balance sheets. In the '70s and '80s, Sears, Roebuck and Co. persisted with its outmoded (but historically successful) retail model despite the abundant evidence that the customer expected more than worn out, poorly merchandised stores. Consequently, boutiques such as The Gap and discounters such as Wal-Mart picked off Sears customers. Although abundant evidence existed to warrant serious change, Sears' senior management insisted on a remedy of fine-tuning the old model. They ignored managers who advocated the concept of boutiques within the same mall but separate from the main store with a different name, upscale merchandise, and higher price points. These boutiques could thereby take advantage of the mother store's operating systems and support to fit the customers' needs. Sears' insistence on maintaining the status quo persisted with only minor adjustments to the old model from the middle of the '70s to the early '90s with record losses and very poor shareholder value.

Market leaders pour money into shoring up old technology, catering to outmoded customers' needs and expectations, at the expense of investigating new technology and social patterns. The rigidity lies in internal policies, ego defenses of managers comfortable with the status quo, and the knowledge that their success exists in the way they have always done business in the "old model," pictured below.

Figure P.1 Inside-out thinking: the organization as an economic institution.

This model was built on the premise that the organization was the center of activity; that it dictated the play or action to a ready and willing external world. Managers had free sway in the selection and placement of employees. Managers decided on what quality of the product meant and what the price should be. Managers decided when and how much to produce. Managers also decided what resources were to be used and how much of these resources would be used.

Today, the pace of change is faster. The challenge of the 21st century will be to grow better. This translates into growing smarter, balancing economic realities with societal expectations. This balancing act will place greater emphasis on the organization as a socioeconomic institution, requiring managers to become outside-in thinkers: stepping outside the organization to look back in.

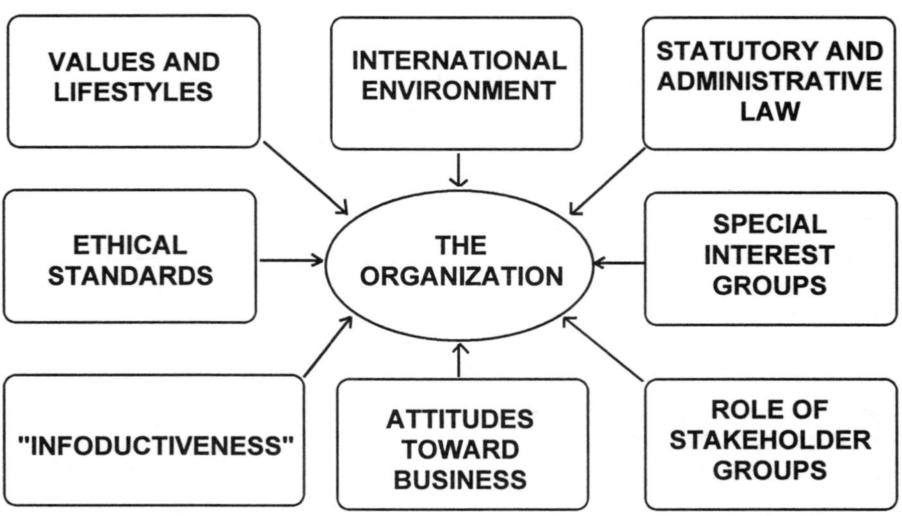

Figure P.2 Outside-in thinking: the organization as a socioeconomic institution.

In this model, managers will need to understand the implications of changes in values and lifestyles, attitudes toward business, statutory and administrative law, roles of special interest groups, stakeholder actions, and business ethics, all taking place in an period of infoductiveness: information reaching a larger, better educated, better informed audience than at any time in the past. Competing in the '90s requires more than business as usual. Leaders in many organizations are looking beyond sharpening their skills in pricing, quality control, innovation, marketing, and service — the inside-out model. They are sharpening their anticipatory skills, which means reviewing what they are doing from an outside-in perspective. They are reconsidering their strategies in an effort to anticipate external activities that affect them.

U.S. business must become more forward looking to deal effectively and systematically with an increasingly turbulent environment. Business organizations face more domestic and international turbulence than ever before. This turbulence has the potential either to destroy companies or to offer them new opportunities. To position companies to deal with change, senior managers must be brought together to assess external initiatives and to review corporate policies in regard to stakeholders, both friendly and hostile. They must constantly check for gaps in the way management thinks things are and the way stakeholders perceive them to be. They must do this before policies become formalized outside the organization. We term this process anticipatory management.

Acknowledgments:

The authors wish to thank

Joel Parthemore
for his help
in editing and formatting this document;
Anthony J. Ashley
for legal and
editing assistance;
Ian Wilson
for making valuable suggestions;
Teresa Yancey Crane
for her ideas and support.

CONTENTS

The Need for Anticipatory Management..................1
Yesterday's Solutions Cause Today's Problem 3
Expensive Wake-Up Calls...6
DysfunctionalResponses..10
Outlook for the '90s..16
Examples of Effective Anticipatory Management..........18
Summary..21

Components of Strategic Thinking.........................23
Models for Managing Organizations..........................26
Traditional, Linear Thinking....................................27
Nine-Dots Problem..29
The Many Worlds of Today's Managers..................31
Strategic Thinking: Nontraditional, Holistic............34
Strategically Placed Holes..38
Summary..42

Surfacing and Challenging Assumptions................43
The Paradigmatic Effect..45
Surfacing Implicit Assumptions...............................47
Examples of Surfaced but Unchallenged
Assumptions...49
Summary..55

Strategic Trend Intelligence System.............................57
Establishing a Strategic Trend Intelligence System.............................59
Defining Terms.............................62
Setting up an Environmental Scanning Workshop.............................65
Other Components of a Strategic Trend Intelligence System.............................67
Case in Point: Repetitive Stress Injuries.............................70
Sources for Scanning.............................72
Pitfalls to Avoid in Establishing and Using a Strategic Trend Intelligence System.............................76
Summary.............................78

The Issue Life Cycle.............................79
The Tyranny of the Small Majority.............................83
Case in Point: The Alar Incident.............................83
The Issue Life Cycle.............................85
A Difficult Lesson to Learn.............................88
Issues of the '70s.............................89
Using the Life Cycle of Issues in Anticipatory Management.............................94
"Infoductiveness".............................99
Summary.............................99

Issues Vulnerability Audit.............................101
Conducting an Audit.............................104
Discovering Strategic Organizational Supports.............................105
Summary.............................109

Issue Briefs.............................111
Anatomy of an Issue Brief.............................113
Summary.............................120

Delphi Rating Method.............................121
Which Category?.............................123
Applying a Tool of the Futurist–The Delphi.............................124
The Delphi Rating Sheet.............................125
Choosing an Owner.............................127
Summary.............................128

The 10-Step Issue Management Process 129
Summary...146

The Issue Accountability Model...........................147
Summary...154

Issue Analysis Work Sheet....................................155

The Scenario Technique Applied to Anticipatory Management...165
The Scenario Technique...167
The Role of Scenarios...167
The "Inner World" of Managers.............................168
Spyglass on the Future...170
Creating Multiple Scenarios: One Approach..........171
A Second Example: Telecommunications..............177
The Product: Multiple Scenario Analysis...............181
Summary...187

The Anticipatory Management Process: Putting It All Together.......................................189
The Anticipatory Management Process..................191
Summary...198

Introducing Anticipatory Management into the Organization..199
Links to Standing Functions...................................202
Industry Institutes and Associations.......................206
The Natural Partnership of Anticipatory Management and TQM.......................................207
Anticipatory Management as Part of Something Bigger...208
Summary...209

Solutions to Anticipatory Management Challenges.....211
The Field Theory.....213
The Lofty Sails Theory.....214
The Boiled Frog Phenomenon.....215
The Monk From the Farthest Temple.....215
The Organization as a Collection of Boutiques.....216
The Functional Foxhole Theory of Management.....217
Management by Problem Solving.....218
Summary.....220

Bibliography.....221

Appendix A: Global Petroleum Trends.....227

Appendix B: Sample Issue Abstract.....231

Appendix C: Sears Taxonomy.....235

Appendix D: Vulnerability Audit Results.....243

Appendix E: Sample Issue Brief.....247

Appendix F: Sample Delphi Rating Sheet and Consensus Report.....253

Appendix G: Case Studies: Issues Management in Action.....259
L.A. Department of Water and Power: Air Quality.....261
Sears, Roebuck and Co.: Regulation of Interstate Commerce.....264
Boeing Corp.....268
Georgia Power Company.....271
Weyerhaeuser Company.....278

Index.....285

CHAPTER ONE

The Need for Anticipatory Management

This handbook describes the techniques of anticipatory management that allow organizations to deal with issues before they reach crisis proportions. Waiting until an issue reaches a crisis, when stakeholders outside the organization have already framed a response, makes difficult work for public affairs to *contain* and public relations to *explain*.

Yesterday's Solutions Cause Today's Problems

As a result of the turbulent '70s and '80s, U.S. business has had to question its strategy, structure, culture, and very purpose. What made for success in the previously protected domestic marketplace does not yield success in a highly charged, unbalanced global marketplace. When they existed in a regulated environment, organizations were able to live with inefficiency for quite some time. They could afford to be reactive instead of proactive. In today's no-holds-barred environment, reactive companies are more likely to falter and fail.

U.S. companies are competing globally against businesses that have inherent advantages, including unregulated natural and human resources, protective laws and taxation policies, less opulent lifestyles, simpler but more restrictive sociopolitical philosophies, and greater economic might. To compete effectively in the future, U.S. businesses must out-think, and out-anticipate, its competitors if they want to out-perform them.

An understanding of anticipatory management will better inform the decision-making hierarchy not only in major corporations, but in government and academic entities as well. Bold initiatives will produce a synthesis of long-term political, economic, and social interests in place of the myopic bureaucratic infighting that characterizes so much of the U.S. political, corporate, and academic scenes. Such initiatives should include partnerships between government, industry, and academia.

Anticipatory actions can lead to market dominance and preemptive positioning. Organizations must balance reactive problem-solving with proactive behavior to avoid problems and discover opportunities.

I. The juggernaut mentality

In the mid-'90s, management's approach to challenges remains a carryover from World War II, characterized by a "juggernaut mentality" that believes in charging forward regardless of outside forces. Problem-solving and crisis-resolution are viewed as the most effective tactical weapons. To resolve a crisis or solve a problem merely results in a return to the point where the organization was beforehand. No competitive leaps will have been achieved; no innovative programs established.

II. Competing in a global economy

This country is competing in a global economy against organizations with well-entrenched anticipatory skills and which operate under tax policies that encourage growth. These competitors are eminently better positioned to succeed in a global marketplace. Until we can out-anticipate them in the home, the classroom, and the marketplace, we will continue losing the dominance we have enjoyed since World War II.

The erosion indicators are myriad if one looks behind the rhetoric. Markets the U.S. once controlled exclusively, such as automobiles and steel, are now dominated by other nations. Consumer electronics invented here are perfected, manufactured, and marketed by others back to the U.S. Traditional strategic planning is based on forces that are not subject to change. Most planning in this country goes nowhere because the external environment in which it was intended to operate was a "snapshot" of a moment in time and not a "motion picture." Plans tend to be too short-sighted and too inside-out oriented to deal with dynamic external forces.

Change is no longer a characteristic of business; change is the essence of business. The rules are different. Players in the new arena all have different rulebooks, not only on how to play the game but on what constitutes winning, the duration of play, and who their teammates and opponents are. Until we refine our anticipatory skills and achieve broader horizons, a clearer focus on the nation's well-being, and an awareness of our competing social needs rather than a myopic focus on the industry, we are doomed to be the "Johnny come lately" imitators of the New World Order.

III. Reliance on economic forecasts

Economic forecasts have been way off mark. They threaten to sacrifice market dominance and ruin our competitiveness. This handbook presents new, holistic tools that better contribute to understanding change.

Expensive Wake-Up Calls

Following are examples of several industries unprepared for trends and events generated by the external environment. Each demonstrates ignorance of developing trends. The organization's attention was entirely internal. The cost of such short-sightedness can be fatal.

I. The airline industry

In 1980 and early 1981, the airline industry had a number of internal problems with which to deal. It should have anticipated problems arising from deregulation of the industry under the new administration. It was not prepared for the strike by federal workers of the Professional Air Traffic Controllers Organization (PATCO).

Founded in 1968, PATCO had 15,000 members in 1981 (out of only 17,000 controllers licensed at the time). A new three-year contract was to be signed between the government and union in March. There were a number of signals that air traffic controllers were upset with the Federal Aviation Administration's management style. Pilots spoke of this repeatedly in their reports to airline management, but the reports were ignored. PATCO had continually been pushing for higher wages, shorter work weeks, and better working conditions.

The air traffic controllers worked without a contract until early August when they went on strike. To punish the union, the U.S. government fired all 11,500 striking controllers. The government then spent $600 million training new controllers.

The strike badly damaged the airline industry. Flights were immediately reduced almost 25 percent. Third-quarter earnings for all airlines dropped dramatically. Many small commuter airlines closed. Had airline management anticipated the strike and entered the debate with a viable plan, the entire crisis might have been averted.

II. The fast-food industry

In the early '80s, large fast-food companies were among the largest training organizations in the U.S., with many young employees and annual turnover generally above 125 percent. Although they had high turnover, the industry had no problem obtaining entry-level employees and were able to avoid paying long-term benefits. Training new employees was simple and inexpensive. The high attrition rate seemed a cost-effective strategy.

The industry failed to anticipate a significant demographic change that would undermine its employment practice: the population drop in 16-to-18-year-olds. Had it been ready, the industry could have lessened the need for new employees by putting more capital in equipment. Belatedly, some companies developed devices like the clamshell grill which cooks hamburgers on both sides, and a pneumatic tube for shooting the hamburgers to the front, thereby eliminating two or three positions per shift or 10-15 people per month, per outlet.

In response to population trends, the industry has actively sought older, part-time employees; but this has limited crew flexibility (Teenagers leave willingly if there is not enough work on their shift; older employees want to stay.), so employee costs have risen. Anticipatory management might have found innovative alternatives instead of costly reactive strategies.

III. The automobile industry

With the Bronco II fiasco, the Ford Motor Co. management team used inside-out thinking and tried to rationalize it as proactive behavior.

Ford introduced the Bronco II in 1982. As early as 1981, senior management knew that the vehicle was unstable: it tended to roll over on turns. This was confirmed by films of rollover tests, internal reports on changes needed to stabilize the vehicle, and memoranda to top management about marketing concerns. Even after its introduction, Ford tests continued to show the vehicle's tendency to tip on sharp turns. As late as May 1982, a Bronco II rolled over and broke the safety outrigger provided to keep test vehicles from flipping over all the way. Concerned about test-driver safety, Ford suspended further live tests and relied instead on computer simulations.

Ford lawyers played a central role by drafting preventive legal advice to management, keeping track of documents that could be used against the company in court, and writing exculpatory warning labels for user manuals.

According to the Insurance Institute for Highway Safety, more than 260 people have died in Bronco II rollovers.

The company was proactive in accumulating data, but in making exculpatory warning labels its thinking was inside out and bottom line. Anticipatory thinking would have led to directives for redesign. This is a perfect example of a dysfunctional—and deadly—response.

Dysfunctional Responses

The ways of the past will have to change. Business leaders are reacting to issues in dysfunctional ways: either systemically (doing the wrong thing but in the prescribed manner) or tactically (calling in the "fog merchants," waiting to see how big the problem gets, sending the boys to Washington to fix it, staging public relations blitzes, or offering ad hoc responses).

I. Systemic dysfunctional responses

A systemic dysfunctional response results from working harder and doing things faster. Where old solutions are not working, people are not looking for new ideas; they are trying harder to make the old ones work.

What should a manager do? The old model spells out yesterday's solutions clearly: the training, the textbooks, and that time-honored test, the years of experience. If managers use the old model, they may do the wrong thing, but they can claim to be doing it in the proper manner. They are covered.

Senge (1990) calls such fixation on events a myopic view of dealing with change. Many organizations are still concentrating on events: last month's sales, staff cuts, new merchandise promotions, and so on. In the mid '80s senior management at Sears, Roebuck and Co. decided to boost flagging retail sales by establishing "the store of the future." Massive effort in manpower and dollars went into staging the event. Racks were moved, walls painted, advertising touted the event, and special teams of employees were sent in to help out. Customers did not return.

The next response was to fire a few middle managers and one top manager. A subsequent event was staged, using the campaign slogan "everyday low prices" with more mass manpower, more dollars, and more fanfare. The customers still did not return. Several event iterations followed, all nothing more than quick, expensive, ineffective fixes.

Senge believes that the primary threats to corporate survival come from gradual processes like environmental decay, eroding public education, obsolete infrastructure, and declining product quality, not from sudden events. Sears' dilemma was of this sort and could not be overcome by quick fixes. Faced by a slow disaffection of the customer base through lack of a well-considered price-quality-value equation, Sears management did not try to view its trouble from the outside-in perspective.

Sears has brought in outside managers, including a new CEO, and the giant may be starting to turn around. Bringing someone in from outside the present paradigm provided Sears with a fresh look at the retailing business. Only time will tell. It usually does.

The '70s taught a valuable lesson to managers: Learn to survive in a highly turbulent environment of new legislation and regulatory initiatives with constantly shifting societal attitudes and expectations. The alphabet soup of regulatory agencies with license to put a company out of business proliferated. Still many businesses continue to concentrate inward.

There continues to be a great deal of "yes we have the situation under control" statements and heads nodding agreement, but the patient's vital signs are poor. Although organizations like the Business Roundtable flourish and bandaging of some regulatory wounds has helped, the patient's global competitiveness and productivity are flagging.

Most managers were trained in, by, and for a domestic industrial economy, but are now forced to function in a global information and service economy. The reliance on linear progressions, hierarchical structures, ensured promotions, and rewards tied to industrial production standards are no longer appropriate.

II. Tactical dysfunctional responses

Another testing ground for anticipatory management lies in confronting the limitations and possible demise of kamikaze lobbying techniques, the grass-roots lobbying used by so-called fog and spin merchants. Perot referred to this group in his '92 campaign as "the boys with the $1,000 suits and the alligator shoes."

No more classic example of kamikaze lobbying exists than the attempt by plastic surgeons to influence the Food and Drug Administration (FDA) in the battle over breast implants. Rather than attempting to work with the FDA to find answers, their approach, using a $2 million war chest, was to attack FDA head David Kessler and investigate his wife. They called Kessler a headline-seeking regulator predisposed to banning the devices. They hired Kessler's friends to influence him to reconsider his position. They hired lobbyists to approach Kessler's superiors. They also used traditional tactics of parading a few satisfied customers for public view and appealing for freedom of choice. Finally, an advisory board of medical doctors recommended that the FDA allow the devices to stay on the market without restrictions while the manufacturers conducted more research.

These kamikaze efforts were unsuccessful. Dow Corning Corporation's internal documents became public, suggesting that Dow, the biggest implant maker, had covered up evidence of possible dangers and discouraged its scientists from conducting additional research. Consequently, a federal court in California awarded a woman $7.3 million in damages because her implant ruptured. By early 1994, Dow Corning Corporation had been named in about 9,000 law suits filed by women who say they suffered a number of ailments stemming from their breast implants (*Chicago Tribune,* January 16, 1994, p. 4).

This does not mean that all kamikaze lobbying is wrong. It does mean that where time is limited, options are limited, which may lead lobbyists to be less virtuous. John Adams defined "virtue" as "a passion for the public good." The Japanese take a similar view to long-range planning when they ask: "What is in the best interest of society?" Then they proceed to plan for it, sometimes in 100-year cycles.

Although the vast army of lobbyists, consultants, law firms, public relations wizards, and special interest groups has grown exponentially, the ground swell of public disaffection is also growing.

Wait to see how big it gets

The wait-and-see approach in a tactical response means sitting back and letting things happen then attempting, with a great deal of money and time, to counter controls being mandated from outside. This approach requires less money for intelligence, but the liabilities are enormous: as the available time shrinks, costs rise steeply. U.S. Representative John Dingell (D., Michigan) put it well:

> *Whenever the public outcry there ought to be a law becomes overwhelming, the industry has a very simple choice. Either the folks who know the industry can fashion, in a timely manner, a program to correct the problem or we in Congress, who know much less about the industry, will probably do it for you.*

Send the boys to Washington to fix it

The send-the-boys-to-Washington approach is another too-little, too-late attempt to avoid taking charge. Without proper intelligence, public affairs staffs are not aware of an issue until it appears in the Federal Register or until their legislative tracking service alerts them to a bill. Once an issue reaches the policy agenda stage, little can be done. The most that weeping and wailing, money and time can achieve is perhaps a line change in the bill.

Public relations blitzes

Public relations blitzes are reactive. Corporate flag waving, slick advertising, and fancy speeches do little to resolve issues.

Firestone's Radial 500 tire is a classic example. In 1978, the government accused Firestone of selling a line of defective tires. According to federal authorities and industry insiders, the Radial 500 tire was prone to blowouts, tread separation and other dangerous wear factors. There were thousands of consumer complaints.

Prudence lost out to short-term profitability. The company's stonewalling allowed it to continue selling the tire. Firestone attempted traditional PR blitzes, even hiring actor Jimmy Stewart as a spokesperson. Eventually, Firestone had to recall the tire and pay $135 million in damages.

Corporate behavior of this kind has caused the public to grow skeptical. The lack of public credibility results in millions of dollars wasted on advertising responding to debates, instead of anticipating and directing them.

Ad hoc programs

Many companies have started ad hoc programs as a tactical response to issues. One such example is the introduction of a minority vendor program, usually inaugurated with a PR blitz. The media is alerted and a person, generally the most articulate and photogenic minority representative available, is selected to head the program. Few resources are allocated;

the function is viewed from within the company as nice but unnecessary.

Outlook for the '90s

The need for anticipatory skills has never been greater. The Institute for Crisis Management's forecast for the remainder of the '90s calls for industrial accidents and other operational crises to decline in importance. Top management decisions in both profit and non-profit organizations will be subject to more scrutiny by the media, focusing on questionable management practices. The government will attend increasingly to environmental hazards and cases of poor product quality, impropriety, criminal behavior, and bad judgment. Guilt or innocence will be determined by the courts of public opinion and not the courts of law. Human resource problems will re-emerge as a source of management difficulties. Recent developments in cases of sexual harassment and age and sex discrimination will heighten the predicament.

Consumer groups

Consumer groups will continue to be a force with which to contend. Look for attention on animal rights, abortion rights, and worker rights. The growing sophistication of various stakeholders is a reason to pay attention to diverse views. They have larger bank accounts, better databases, and the luxury usually to concentrate on a single issue.

Whistle blowing

Among the major players for the '90s are the whistle blowers — employees who report what they perceive to be illegal activities by the company. The Institute for Crisis Management suggests that with a possible 15 percent to 20 percent bounty called for by the federal False Claim Act, more employees will opt to blow the whistle. Woe to the company that first finds out about a serious problem when a lawsuit is filed and distributed to the media by an employee's attorney or the government.

Whistle Blower Awarded $13 million

Cincinnati-A federal judge has awarded $13.5 million to the man who blew the whistle on the Israeli bribery scheme involving General Electric Co.

This is the largest such award ever granted under the U.S. False Claims Act. A company spokesperson...

Examples of Effective Anticipatory Management

A number of corporate giants have used anticipatory management to minimize the impact of issues on profits and to preserve their image.

United Airlines

In 1986, senior managers at United Airlines knew their customer service was slipping at a time when quality service was seen by other industries as crucial. Yet the chief executive officer (CEO) believed that improved service meant more employees and a less efficient operating system. No senior manager dared mention the problem.

The anticipatory management process allowed the service ethic issue to be addressed in an issue brief, saying not how neglectful United's service was but how successful other organizations had been. The nine-member steering committee unanimously rated a renewed service ethic as a top priority. Not one of these individuals would have raised the issue alone.

During the issue evaluation phase it was revealed that United's advertising promoted something not being delivered; dissatisfaction arose from what the customer was led to expect. United's advertisements featured 21-year-old flight attendants on big, wide-body jets. In reality the average age of a flight attendant was 37 years. Attendants were shown serving coffee in china, fluffing pillows, and hanging garment bags for passengers. The real-world passenger rarely received these amenities. Between the regulations of the Federal Aviation Administration and the union, attendants had neither time nor encouragement to do these things.

It took an off-site, cross-functional evaluation team of senior managers to reveal these blunders. The company was promising what it had no capacity to deliver. Possible solutions were shaped into an action plan and approved by the CEO. The cold light of analysis, away from the cozy vantage point of the foxhole, made the need for action obvious. Ironically through the evaluation of the issue and the development of an action plan, none of the CEO's original concerns manifested themselves.

Royal Dutch Shell

By training managers to see issues from multiple perspectives and reevaluate their mind-sets, Royal Dutch Shell saved billions of dollars that other oil companies lost as a result of the 1973 and 1979 oil crises. How did they dothis?

Shell's planners felt that some oil-producing countries were making more money than they could use. The leaders of these countries knew that oil was a finite resource. When it ran out, they would lose their income. Conventional industry wisdom held that oil was cheap and plentiful, and that oil-producing countries were so competitive and so suspicious of each other that they could never work together to restrict output. The idea that they could raise the price of oil and that not one of the countries would undercut the price was unthinkable.

Shell's planners produced an unlikely sounding scenario: Oil-producing nations would form a cartel and raise the price of oil. They were able to bring to their managers a view of the future different from what conventional wisdom suggested. The managers were forced to identify and question all of their implicit assumptions.

When the OPEC embargo became reality, Shell managers responded differently from other oil companies. They changed their refinery investment strategy, oil field location strategy, and demand forecasts. Rather than "circling the wagons" or becoming more centralized, they gave their operating companies more freedom to move. Shell increased their global market share by 8 percent within two years.

McDonald's

In 1983, McDonald's Corporation undertook the largest toy recall ever, a recall that went unnoticed by the public. Shortly after establishing an anticipatory management program in 1981 that required all senior executives from the CEO down to be involved, the company discovered a possible choking hazard for children in a toy collection it planned to promote.

Although the toy had passed the Consumer Product Safety Commission's standards, a private laboratory employed by the company found that the toy would break when struck repeatedly in one place, producing a small piece on which a child might choke. Good corporate citizenship dictated that the toy could not be released. A few parents were upset and some licensees were concerned about lost sales — small costs compared to releasing a potentially hazardous product.

Summary

The rules of the management game have fundamentally changed. These new values must be accompanied by new ways of dealing with issues. This handbook provides detailed, interwoven, step-by-step methodologies to help today's managers deal more effectively with change. It illustrates the importance of introducing new methods of strategic thinking, challenging ingrained assumptions, and confronting the external forces that affect business. The next chapter introduces the concept of strategic thinking, the bedrock of using anticipatory management tools to achieve excellence.

CHAPTER TWO

Components of Strategic Thinking

Strategic planning is a lot like jogging. It is not an effective way to get someplace, but if you do it often enough you feel better.

Tom Peters, author of many books on excellence and strategy, McGill University professor Henry Mintzberg, and others, are peeling the death knell for strategic planning. They refer to the mindless love affair with planning over the last 30 years that Tom Peters argues effectively ended when Jack Welch, GE chairman, shut down GE's hyper-formalized planning system. Mintzberg's book, *The Rise and Fall of Strategic Planning,* articulates the arguments that many managers have known for years but were unable to mention because it was not politically correct.

The focus of most strategic plans was on process and was an extension of industrial psychologists' attempts to systematize the work place. This process orientation grew from the time and motion work of Frederick Taylor who contributed to the industrial revolution. This lock-step, process thinking was fine for the slow-to-change industrial period. In the fast-paced changes of the '90s, however, it is essentially strangling innovation and decision-making.

Mintzberg points out that planning, by its very nature, defines and preserves categories. There has been a fundamental separation of the manager from the plan, a sort of disassociation of thinking from acting. Strategic thinking puts the emphasis on involving the manager and encourages creativity in regards to the resources and assets at the manager's disposal. This creativity allows the manager to see new categories and provides the opportunity to rearrange and recluster old categories.

Strategic thinking insists that the hierarchical models established to fill the needs of the industrial revolution must give way to newer more flexible arrangements.

Models for Managing Organizations

The standard model for managing organizations has its origins in structures established by the pharaohs and adopted by the military. This hierarchical model pictures a general sitting high on a hill, setting strategy for troops in the field below. Each unit commander is given a specific responsibility on the assumption that if each accomplishes his objectives, the war will be won.

Transferring this model to corporate America, one substitutes tall office buildings for hills, but the concept is the same. The management subculture requires that higher echelons arrange the division of labor among employees and otherwise dictate how work is organized. They alone decide who should select and train workers.

Traditional, Linear Thinking

The underlying assumption is that subdivision makes complex tasks manageable. The reality is that a programmer working for a large organization will work on one piece of a larger program and have no sense of contributing to the overall picture.

Many managerial assignments work similarly. A manager only works on portions of the overall corporate plan. During the industrial revolution such division of labor was successful because tasks were relatively simple, lead times were long, and no one was doing things differently. The model worked well for producing widgets. To train the laboring masses, educators taught the basics: reading, writing, and arithmetic.

Beneath this overt curriculum lay an invisible, far more basic one consisting of punctuality, obedience, and rote work. This mass education model produces pliable, regimented workers well-suited to the demands of industrial technology and the assembly line. It also produces managers who fit the hierarchical management strategy where information flows up and down a well-defined organizational ladder.

Consequences of Linear Thinking

Using this model, organizations select and promote managers based on obedience and intelligence. In career considerations, extensive use is made of intelligence tests, which place a high priority on memorization and linear thinking (solving puzzles, sorting data, detecting obscure relationships) in processing large amounts of material. Through early training and reward systems, intelligence is defined in terms of linear thought patterns.

Linear thinkers translate success and survival into an ever more rigid adherence to plans that stress control of every detail. Policies are rigorously spelled out so that everyone knows exactly what to do in every circumstance. These policies only marginally attempt to anticipate contingencies. Incremental approaches are encouraged, complacency sets in, and strategic thinking (which allows managers to "step outside themselves") is discouraged.

Advocates of ambitious strategies that do not seem to reflect linear thought patterns may find themselves sidelined, labeled as mavericks. In most organizations the rewards go to those skilled at maintaining the status quo. Success is tied closely to an ability to conform to the organizational culture. Because that culture exalts logic and rationality, analysts, rather than innovators, get ahead.

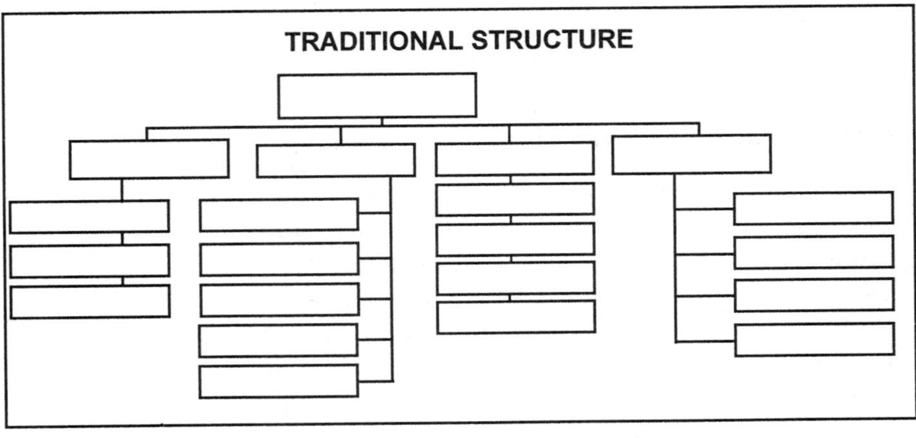

Figure 2.1 The traditional organizational structure emphasizes linear thinking.

Nine-Dots Problem

A familiar puzzle requiring non-linear thinking is shown below. The task is to connect all nine dots with four straight, connected lines. When presented with this challenge, many people will struggle vainly, trapped within the limits created by the nine dots and within the limits of their problem-solving techniques. The solution requires "stepping outside the box," as you will see on the next page.

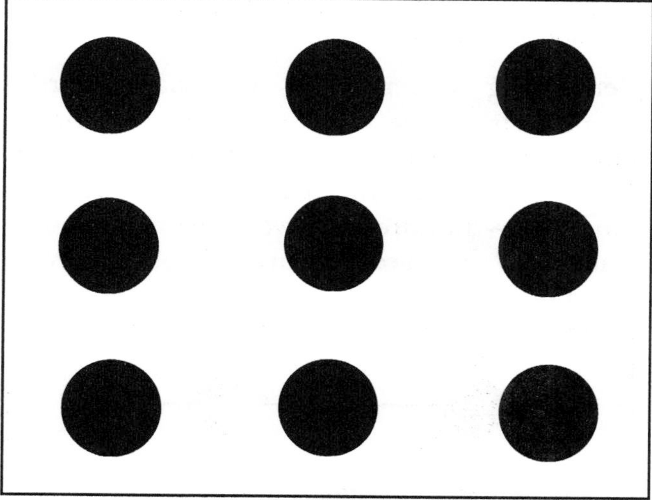

Figure 2.2 The Nine Dots Puzzle

Connect the nine dots with four lines without *ever* lifting pencil from paper.

Modern business reality demands non-linear, outside-the-box thinking. It is no longer possible to function effectively within the old model. U.S. industries are having to adjust to demands for workplace empowerment. The wars (now economic, not political) are bigger and fought on many fronts simultaneously. There are more enemies who are more sophisticated and who fight by different rules. The armies vary in size and deployment.

Business must move from the industrial models of yesterday to the models needed in a post-industrial, information-based economy. Tomorrow's organizations will put less emphasis on hierarchies and more on networks. They will be perpetually self-reorganizing, more akin to biological systems.

Networking depends on informal, interdependent structures. Networks transcend organizational boundaries in executing their missions. That is precisely the benefit of a network situation — hundreds of work teams linked to managers who are encouraged to think strategically.

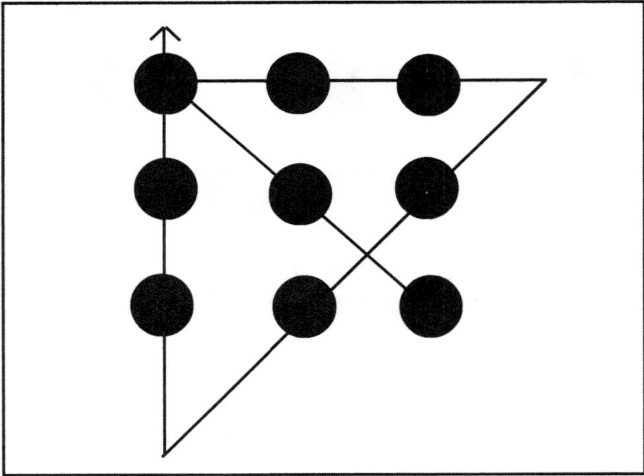

Figure 2.3 Nine-dots solution

The Many Worlds of Today's Managers

For years, managers were kept insulated and isolated inside the organization. Their responsibilities were narrowly-defined. They were expected to think only of their immediate area of responsibility. Their areas of discretion were limited by tightly-written job descriptions. Little deviation was allowed. It was someone else's job to think about the bigger picture, but it was never really clear to the manager *who* that someone was.

This structure kept the organization in control. But it tended to shape managers' attitudes in negative ways. They learned to do what they were told and little more. They avoided conflict with their bosses. They avoided additional responsibility, forcing their bosses to sign off on decisions they themselves could make. This structure fostered a schoolyard sullenness where bosses played the role of disciplinarians and their direct-reports played the role of scolded children.

Times have changed. All managers are now required to deal with the macro-world outside their organization. This requires new skills, behaviors and understandings. Instead of focusing on what their superior is thinking, managers must focus on the shifts and changes in the macro-world (see Figure 2.4) and what they imply for the organization. Managers must also empower their direct-reports to do the same.

Shifts and changes in the macro-world are important because the forces that comprise this space — social, economic, technological, political,

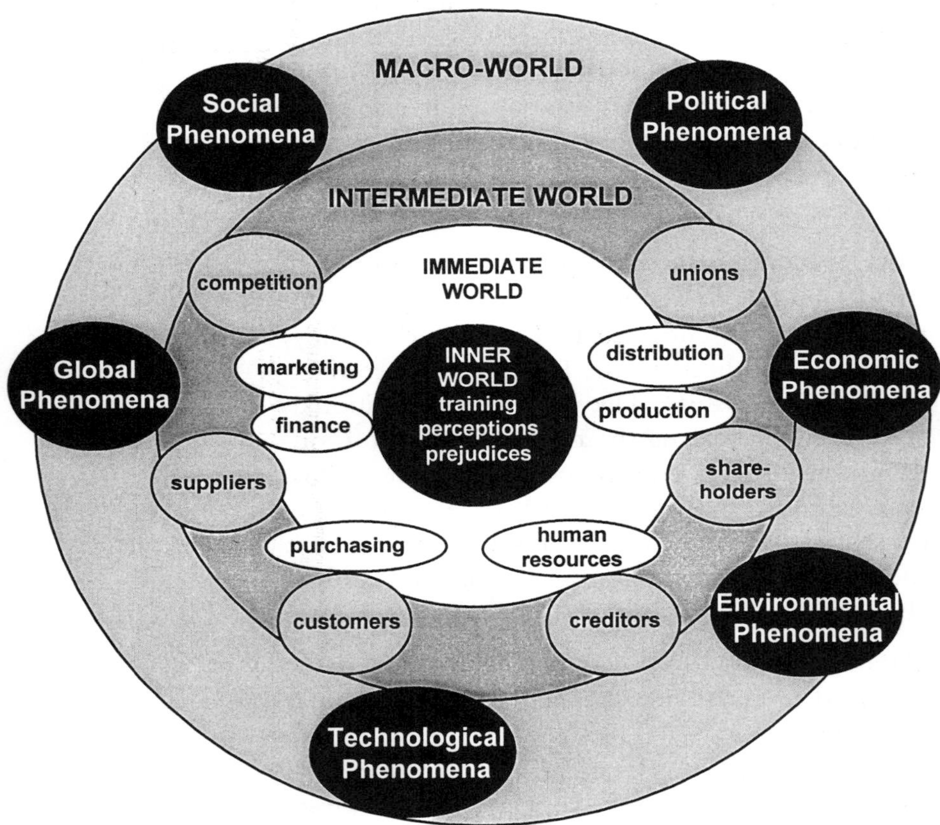

Figure 2.4 The many worlds of the manager.

global and environmental phenomena — interact to reverberate through the intermediate world of the manager. This, in turn, causes shifts in the manager's immediate world. These changes, many of which are at one time evolutionary and at other times revolutionary, have to be dealt with in the manager's inner-world.

Evolutionary shifts in the macro-world, such as a shift in birth rates, may not impact today's sales, but may have a profound impact on how money will be spent over the next generation. Thus, a shift in a social phenomenon may create shifts in economic patterns. An event as revolutionary as Three Mile Island will influence social behavior in the form of attitudes toward nuclear power, thus affecting the industry for years into the future.

Managers' interpretations of these phenomena are influenced by their inner-world, the result of training, perceptions, prejudices, and tradition. This inner-world forms a decision screen managers use to interpret information from the outside.

Most business training and business school courses prepare the manager to deal at inner, immediate, and intermediate levels. However, managers are now required to respond to the macro-world and to interpret how the trends, events, and developments in that world might impact the business world. To do this effectively, managers need the tools and techniques of anticipation.

Strategic Thinking: Nontraditional, Holistic

It is not the lofty sails but the unseen wind that moves the ship.

— *W. MacNeile Dixon*

Dixon explains clearly what is happening in the corporate sector. Perspectives are formed from experiences that deal with the sails of management. Although these experiences are important, they do not track the unseen wind that moves the organization in new directions, or off course. Just as navigators had to refine their tools by moving from the sextant to the compass, to the gyrocompass, and on to inertial guidance systems, so, too, will the management navigators of the future have to develop more sophisticated tools.

Our educational system was established to satisfy the needs of the agricultural era and then altered slightly to accommodate the industrial era. Most current organizational models have their roots in the industrial period. We now find ourselves in a post-industrial, information-based economy using the wrong management models.

Ohmae (1982) defines strategic thinking as a marriage of information and insight that allows a clear understanding of each element in a situation. Strategic thinking is used to reorder the elements to maximize results within the emerging context. Because events in the real world seldom fit a linear model, the strategic thinker dissects a situation into its constituent parts and reassembles them into a pattern, based on their significance and their relationship to the desired outcome.

Mintzberg (1994) says that strategic thinking is about a synthesis of intuition and creativity. Strategic thinking offers an integrated perspective on the organization, a not-too-precisely articulated vision of direction.

The Broad Picture

Strategic thinkers look at the broad picture of the organization — its stakeholders, competition, and environment — and respond with a comprehensive set of initiatives. They examine resources in light of opportunities provided by the external environment. They depend on an outside-in perspective, allowing managers to maximize resources. The broad view helps break tunnel vision so that new relationships and new markets become conceivable.

Strategic thinking concentrates on interrelationships rather than individual components, and views organizational surroundings as a "moving picture" rather than a "snapshot." It looks at structures and their supports. Strategic thinking on issues begins with an understanding of the issue's essence. By establishing what the issue is, thoughts focus on achieving a solution for the whole rather than finding remedies for each of the parts, then assuming the issue has been handled.

We tend to think too fast. Tests and other evaluation methods place too great an emphasis on getting an answer quickly. This kind of short-circuited thinking is prevalent in business. Managers identify, plan, and implement, letting the lawyers sort out the problems that result from their knee-jerk behavior.

The complexity of modern business demands a more considered approach. Strategic thinking observes phenomena, determines what relationships exist among them, and groups them into categories that can be evaluated on their significance to the organization. Initiatives are created by managers formulating hypothetical solutions, validating them with in-depth analysis (e.g., scenarios), and transforming them into action plans for implementation by line managers.

Because strategic thinking is entirely creative, partly intuitive, and often disruptive of existing patterns of thought, it has been categorized as right-brain thinking: holistic, non-verbal, spatial. Strategic thinking challenges conventional by-the-numbers wisdom. It challenges the idea of incremental improvement: doing better what is being done already.

Left-brain thinkers thrive where resources are rigorously allocated, the environment predictable, and the organization directed toward meeting budgets and schedules. Most managers have been trained to be conventional thinkers, relying on the left half of their brain.

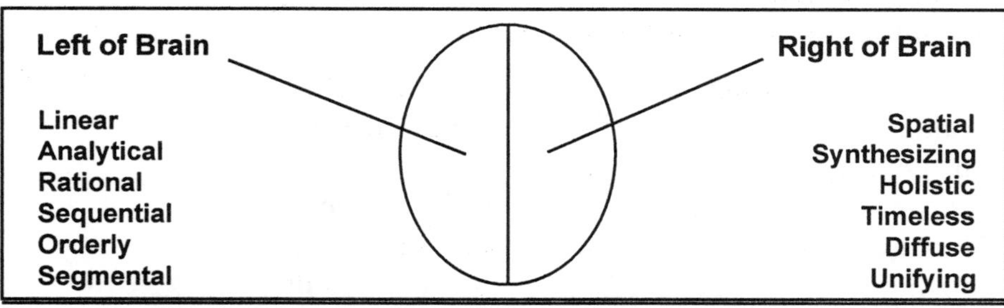

Figure 2.5 Left -vs right-brain thinking.

Successful strategies result not from rigorous analysis of what is and has been, but consideration of what might be. Strategic thinking does not reject analysis. Analysis is used to stimulate creativity, to test the ideas that emerge, to work out the implications of those ideas, and to ensure successful execution of perhaps risky but high-potential ideas that might otherwise never have a chance.

The most successful breakthroughs historically have come through non-linear thinking. The abrupt changes in writing media — the jumps from stylus to pen to typewriter to word processor — were wild-card events. Great strategies, like great works of art or scientific discoveries, call for technical mastery in implementation but originate in insights that go beyond formal, rational, conscious analysis. Strategic thinking may appear at odds with the organizational culture. How can a habit-bound bureaucratic organization gain the capacity to be creative?

In a competitive world, survival depends on managers working a dual role. On the one hand, they must be strategists, giving free rein to their entrepreneurial flair to produce bold and imaginative ideas. On the other hand, they are asked to analyze ideas, prioritize them, and share successful ones with the rest of the organization. Managers of the future will need to be pragmatic dreamers.

Holism vs. Reduction

Most corporate thinking is reductionist, attempting to reduce each challenge to component parts and then passing out responsibility for them to members of the management team. The assumption is that members will receive their piece of the puzzle, return to their department, and solve their piece. A master overseer puts all the pieces together to solve the problem. Attempting to assemble such fragmented solutions is like putting Humpty Dumpty together again.

Simplifying complex problems by breaking them into manageable pieces has costly drawbacks. An enormous amount of time and energy is expended as the price of obtaining new business. No competitive breakthroughs occur while the organization is in repairs mode. By viewing a problem as its component parts, the view of the whole may be lost.

Strategically Placed Holes

The Bigger and Deeper Trap

A useful characterization of left- and right-brain thinking is that with the left brain, logic is in control; whereas, with the right brain, logic is at the service of the mind. Logic is a tool used to dig holes deeper and bigger. If the hole is in the wrong place, no amount of digging is going to put it right.

Many businesses find themselves with very big, very deep holes that are in the wrong place. As discussed earlier, in the mid-'80s Sears found itself with a bulky, unprofitable catalog business and a retail structure that was not meeting customer needs. Sears responded by introducing its "store of the future" (which was more of the same with new fixtures) and "everyday low pricing" (which was more of the same with some reduced prices). Sears management was digging the traditional department store hole deeper, rather than rethinking the business to reach new customers. Recently, senior managers have been brought in from outside the Sears family with ideas that are bringing customers back.

IBM long emphasized mainframes over personal computers (PCs) and software, resulting in substantial losses and isolation from the growing software and PC end of the business. Kenneth Olsen, CEO of Digital Equipment Corp. (DEC), also was unwilling to believe in a future for PCs. DEC also focused on large computer systems and was slow to enter the lucrative PC market. Hole-digging cost Olsen and IBM CEO John Akers their jobs.

In each case, the company became more efficient at what it was doing wrong. Rather than digging a new hole in a new place, the old one was dug deeper. Why?

The Well-Trod Path

Managers are reluctant to abandon holes in which they have a great deal of investment. They apply the faster, harder, longer, deeper approach in an attempt to alleviate the situation. It is difficult to find a different location by looking harder in the same direction. But enlarging an existing hole offers immediate rewards and the promise of future achievement. There is comfort in a familiar, well-worked hole. The more expert one becomes with a particular hole, the less likely one is to jump out of it. In-house experts can usually be found at the bottom of the deepest holes. One might call this truly inside-out thinking!

The hole analogy suggests why major corporations have been caught off-guard by impending shifts in the environment. When they did notice, they ignored what did not relate directly to their holes. Even if the shifts did relate directly and suggested a different location or links to other holes, managers would do nothing without some type of directive.

The Sustainable Advantage

A maxim of management is "no surprises." Yet management sayings like "Keep your nose to the grindstone;" "Keep your head down and charge;" "Follow the puck;" "The only way to get ahead in this company is to be steeped in the business;" and, "It can't possibly be worthwhile or we would have thought of it," lead to guaranteed, unpleasant surprises to many organizations.

The pace of change, or more importantly, the perceived pace of change, is far higher in the present *technological* revolution than it was in the industrial revolution. As Figure 2.6 demonstrates, the technological revolution will accomplish in one-forth the time what it took the industrial revolution to accomplish. Added to the faster

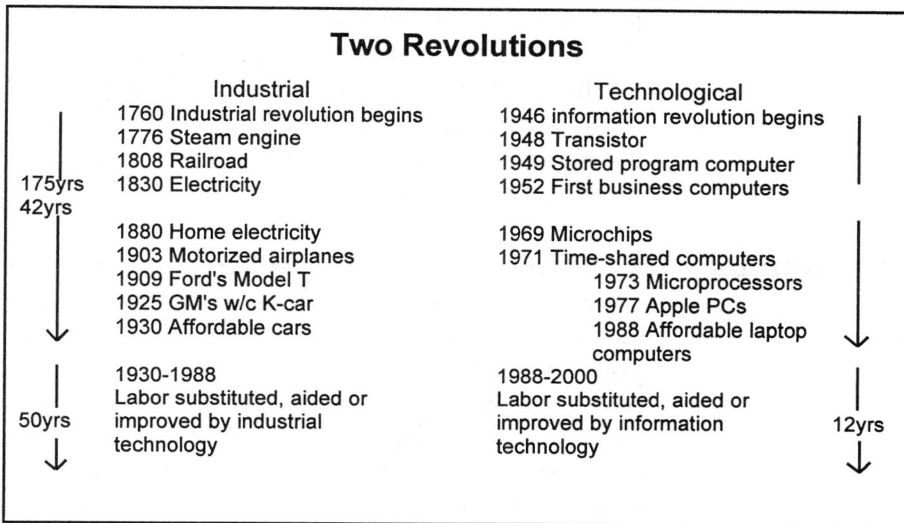

Figure 2.6 The pace of change. Modified from Makridakis, Spyros.*Forecasting, Planning and Strategy for the 21st Century*.

pace of change is the ease of entry into many industries. In the past it took large amounts of money and many years to get into the automobile, steel, electronics, or housing business. The time from start up to mega-business has shrunk in some cases to little more than a decade — witness Bill Gates and Microsoft.

The decreasing limitations of national boundaries will require managers to adjust to external forces far more quickly. Where once many industries were dominated by a single leader — computers (IBM), automobiles (General Motors), photography (Eastman Kodak), department retail (Sears), photocopying (Xerox) — competition has become diverse and the playing field uneven. U.S. companies are vulnerable to European companies that are vulnerable to

Japanese companies that are vulnerable to the Koreans. The Koreans will soon be vulnerable to the Vietnamese. Encouraging managers to think strategically, get outside their holes or boxes, and synthesize new ideas may be the only sustainable competitive advantage.

Summary

The military model based on having one brilliant general — a Ford, Wood, Kroc, Sloan, Watson, or Patton — is no longer workable. It is just not possible any longer to strategize from the top and have everyone else follow orders. Life was simpler when the generals did their thing. But the greatest accomplishments await the organizational structures and management tools that are only now arising. Chapters 3 through 12 describe the 10 power tools of the new era.

CHAPTER THREE

Power Tool Number One

Surfacing and Challenging Assumptions

We use implicit assumptions, deeply ingrained frames of reference, mental mind sets, and other understandings about the world in which we operate when making decisions and taking action. Collectively, these predisposed assumptions form a paradigm.

A paradigm is, broadly construed, the set of those beliefs, axioms, assumptions, givens or fundamentals that order and provide coherence to our picture of what reality is and how it works. These beliefs are like our map of reality. They are not reality itself, but the directions we use to find our way across the terrain

— Ogilvy and Schwartz, 1979.

Paradigms are the lenses through which we perceive the outside world. They explain the environment and help us anticipate others' behavior. They constitute our intelligence, our understanding of the world and ourselves.

The Paradigmatic Effect

The paradigmatic effect is a contributing force in the failure of managers to recognize change. Managers' mind-sets are formed from an accumulation of assumptions developed over time, leading to an internalized map of reality, a decision screen through which to filter information. Whole industries can become myopic because of their adherence to the prevailing paradigm. New information is rejected that runs counter to these beliefs. The implicit assumptions behind an organization's paradigm shape the company's understanding of itself and drive its strategic planning. Failure to reckon with assumptions is understandable in a stable world where competition takes place between companies whose managers, educated in the same schools, make use of the same consultants who read the same publications. Paradigms are useful and even necessary when each year is essentially like the last. They allow the efficient flow of information and the assimilation of individuals into the culture.

In a turbulent world, failure to challenge implicit assumptions leads to strategic blindness. Long-term success in the modern, no-holds barred world comes to depend on finding and challenging assumptions. Implicit assumptions — decision screens — facilitate the decision making process. Critical assumptions are made over time about pricing, supply, costs, markets, legislation, competition, resources, and — most importantly — stakeholders. Only information that supports these assumptions is allowed through the screen. Information that goes counter to accepted beliefs is rejected or, worse, ignored.

Paradigms are learned from experiences in the organization, either through formal training or by grasping "the way things are done around here." They are embedded in organizational language and culture. Individuals functioning within the paradigm rarely realize that their behavior is being influenced by subtle, unstated assumptions about their environment. Promotion requires being steeped in all aspects of the organizational culture; above all one does not question directives. As a result, companies become castles surrounded by high walls and moats, wherein information about what is going on, both inside and outside the walls, is self-corroborating.

The Boiled Frog Phenomenon

Scientists make reference to the fact that a frog, when placed in a beaker of cold water that is gradually heated, will become quite comfortable at first. However, when the temperature of the water becomes hot enough to boil or kill it, the frog is too weak to do what is necessary to escape its fate. In business, external phenomenon are similar to the heat being applied to the beaker, warm at first — but deadly if conditions are not changed.

Surfacing Implicit Assumptions

Traditionally, environmental challenges are met with a reactive crash-program mentality. Managers resist becoming more anticipatory, even though it would provide the lead time to keep costs down and plan more effectively for an uncertain future. They are understandably scared of change.

Managers need lead time to identify, understand, and adapt to external forces. Figure 3.1 demonstrates the time-cost trade-off. An issue surfaced at T1(time 1) is dealt with at C1(cost 1). When an issue is allowed to progress to T2 it must be paid for at C2, which is at a substantially higher cost. The difference between C1 and C2 is lead time. Lead time allows the organization the opportunity to think through implications and challenges before they become critical. Lead time is the margin that anticipatory skills can provide. Managers must anticipate consequences in order to develop well-considered policies. Lead time can change emerging issues from threats to opportunities.

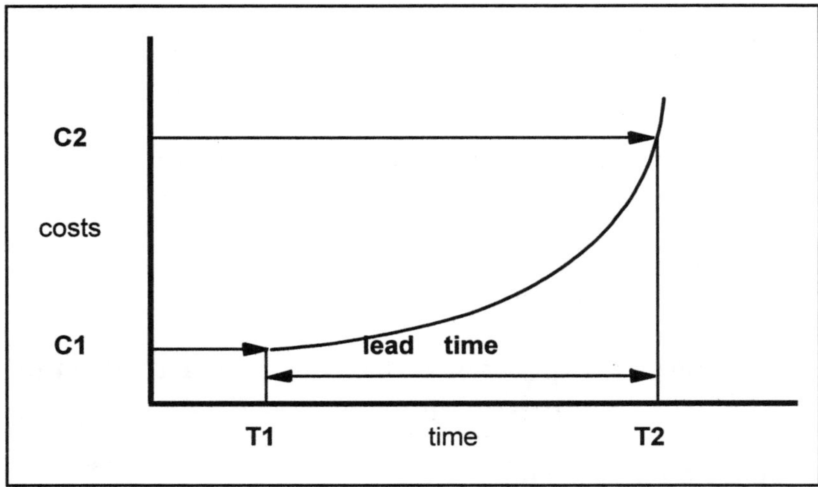

Figure 3.1. The time-cost trade off.

If managers do not periodically surface and examine their assumptions about the business they are in, they are vulnerable to changes in the marketplace. Every time managers ignore this advice, they lose customers.

Outside-in thinking helps management maintain flexible filtering. Managers step outside the organization to look back in. They ask, "How will emerging trends affect our business?" Where industries have not moved from paradigm rigidity to paradigm pliancy, they become victims of their assumptions as the rate of change accelerates.

Examples of Surfaced but Unchallenged Assumptions

The U.S. automobile industry

Auto manufacturing has been so successful in this country that the guiding principles of its early success became implicit operating assumptions. The industry's critical assumptions as it entered the '70s included:

- We are in the business of making money, not cars.
- Strict centralized financial controls are the secret to good administration.
- The American car market is isolated from the rest of the world. Foreign competition will not exceed 15 percent of the domestic market.
- Energy will always be cheap and abundant.
- Workers are expendable and do not have an impact on productivity.
- Cars are primarily symbols; styling is more important than quality to buyers who will trade up every other year.
- Managers should be promoted from within.
- The consumer movement does not represent the concerns of a significant portion of the American public.
- Success comes from having the resources to adopt others' innovations quickly.

Although there was nothing intrinsically wrong about these assumptions in the early '70s, they were beginning to lose their validity during the late '70s because the global environment was changing. After the 1973 oil embargo, gasoline prices escalated, Japanese automobiles invaded U.S. shores, consumer values shifted from style to quality, families shrank, workers' attitudes changed, and dealings with government required cooperation and acceptance of interference.

Have other U.S. industries learned anything from Detroit? The answer must be a resounding, "No!" Consider the recent crises in steel, banking, consumer electronics, chemicals, and nuclear energy. Unless U.S. business becomes more flexible in dealing with its environment, it can anticipate further loss.

The steel industry

The steel industry's assumptions at the time of the 1973 oil embargo included:

- American producers are more efficient than foreigners.
- The U.S. is shielded from foreign competition.
- American steel plants are the most advanced in the world.
- Cost-of-living adjustments (COLAs) are fair trade-offs for pledges of no strikes.
- Cars and appliances will continue to provide a large market for steel.
- Steel will recapture the beverage can market.
- Domestic preference for American steel will continue.
- Plant conditions are sufficient to meet demand.

Many of these assumptions were heavily reinforced by consultants. Industry experts predicted a worldwide steel shortage. Corporate executives asked Congress for billions of dollars in investment tax credits for plant expansions.

Studies were available (Magaziner, 1989) to indicate that foreign steel producers were not only more efficient than their American counterparts, but so much more efficient that they could beat American prices even after paying shipping and customs duties. When Magaziner attempted to explain the facts to steel executives, they refused to listen. One steel executive told Magaziner, "Look son, I was over in Korea during the war. It's not easy to make good steel. Those guys aren't going to be able to do it. I think you're overreacting." Another said, "Every industry expert in the country is predicting a shortage. You don't know what you're talking about." Industry executives and consultants talked only with one another, reinforcing a comfortable but obsolete perspective. The predicted steel shortage, in reality, turned into a surplus, spurred by a decline in the use of steel and a huge increase in production plants. Plastic was fast becoming a substitute for steel. Developing countries expanded their exports, and traditional steel markets (e.g., automobiles) used less steel. U.S. production dropped from 121 million tons in 1973, to 79 million tons in 1987.

The U.S. housing industry

For years, studies have shown a pent-up housing demand. Reliable estimates suggest the

U.S. is presently two million homes under market demand. Is the housing industry mesmerized by unchallenged assumptions? The industry's critical assumptions as it entered the '80s included:

- Home building will always be labor intensive.
- Suppliers will always be dispersed.
- Mortgage rates are the primary cause of builders' problems.
- On-site construction is the only way to produce houses.
- The buyer must come to the builder.
- The product should be aimed at a broad market.
- The needs of the home buyer have not changed in several decades.

Given such assumptions, is it any wonder the industry is ripe for change? Both the English and Japanese are poised to move on this window of opportunity.

In 1979, British home builder Barratt Development, PLC, astonished shoppers at a Sears store in San Diego. While wandering among underwear, lawnmowers, insurance displays, and financial presentations, they came across a fully furnished, full-scale condominium! The price tag was below the U.S. average as well as most dwellings available in the California market.

Having transformed the British building industry with strategies he is now using in California (direct sales, low prices, and tightly defined market segments), Mr. Barratt thinks he can capture a major share (10 percent or more) of the California housing market by the late '90s. If successful, he would become the largest home builder in the U.S. He plans to expand into other Sunbelt states.

The second largest builder in Japan, Missawa Homes, Inc., produces 29,000 homes per year. With scientific precision, Missawa creates a Western-style home, customized to buyers' specifications, in 40 minutes or less using an automated assembly line. The houses are high quality, competitively priced, earthquake- and typhoon-proof, and come with a 10-year warranty. They are complete with home furnishings and appliances. With the help of a computer, the customer has about 2,000 options available. The home can be erected in as little as a day-and-a-half.

In late 1990, Chicago newspapers reported that as many as three of Japan's largest housing manufacturers were actively seeking locations to establish themselves in the U.S. Japanese builders view the U.S. as a country where land is cheap and competition unsophisticated.

Seiko: paradigm pliancy in action

After analyzing trends within the watch business, Seiko, Japan's leading watchmaker, saw the need for a paradigm shift. In the face of changing consumer needs, a worldwide glut of watches, a decline in sales, a lack of product diversity, and shifting market shares, Seiko redefined itself and entered the small precision instruments business. It is now marketing computers, printers, paperback book-sized TVs, and other hi-tech instruments.

The global petroleum industry

Anticipatory management tools and techniques were used by the authors at a 1994 seminar/workshop with managers from a multinational petroleum company, including surfacing the assumptions these managers held about their business. They are as follows:

- Petroleum will remain the major source of world energy.
- Growth in Southeast Asia means growth in petroleum demand, not electricity.
- The company can continue to purchase the crude and refined product it needs.
- The company will continue to be the market leader.
- Refineries will continue to upgrade to meet environmental quality requirements.
- Economic growth is expected to maintain at a 3 percent increase per year and the growth is in Asian countries.
- Crude oil supply is limited, and located in unstable countries (70 percent in Middle East).
- China will emerge as a new superpower economically, politically, and militarily.

- Crude oil prices will range between US$16-20 per barrel for the next 10 years.
- Continued political instability will exist in Asia.
- Alternative fuels will not impact traditional fuel supplies.
- High market growth is expected at 7 percent.
- Demand will be in excess of refining capacity.
- Increased demand will exist for high quality, high-tech products.
- Deregulation will continue.
- Crude supplies are limited.

Summary

There is little question that the '90s will see more complex issues raised by a broader, more organized array of stakeholders, most with a single-issue focus and many well financed. Organizations that give stakeholders the prerogative in framing the issues of the '90s will continue in a fire-fighting, damage control mode. Managers must use a Strategic Trend Intelligence System to identify potentially troublesome emerging issues. The next chapter explains how.

CHAPTER FOUR

Power Tool Number Two

Strategic Trend Intelligence System

...For knowing afar of the evils that are brewing, they are easily cured. But when, for want of such knowledge, they are allowed to grow until everyone can recognize them, there is no longer any remedy to be found.

— *Niccolo Machiavelli,* The Prince, *1531*

The first step in anticipatory management is to identify emerging issues, which requires an intelligence system to provide the organization with crucial information. This chapter considers how to build, maintain, and use a strategic trend intelligence system.

Establishing a Strategic Trend Intelligence System

The means for systematically evaluating the global environment is sometimes referred to as a "strategic trend intelligence system." A relatively new idea being employed by a few companies in the U.S. and abroad, strategic trend intelligence systems systematically track trends and events in the external environment. The system depends on a comprehensive scanning program for basic information, and issues management support for transforming that information into useful intelligence. It offers organizations the lead time they need to adjust swiftly as trends stray from the path of conventional wisdom.

Strategic trend intelligence systems depend upon the ability to scan, monitor and create scenarios. This three-pronged approach is likened to a three-legged stool (Wilson, 1994, personal communication). As with a three-legged stool, this approach provides balance and breadth to insure the widest sweep through the use of scanning. Scanning is regarded as a tracking or monitoring system which follows strategically significant trends, and the creative ability to articulate those trends into scenarios that assist in identifying issues (Fig 4.1).

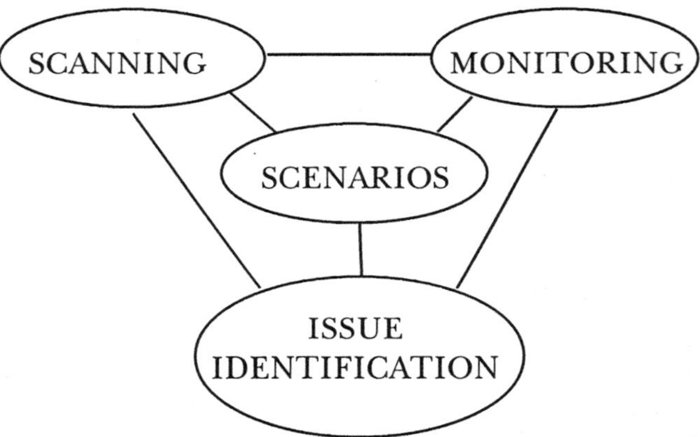

Figure 4.1 Strategic Trend Intelligence System.

Brown and Weiner (1985) define environmental scanning as "a kind of radar to scan the world systematically and signal the new, the unexpected, the major, and the minor." Aguilar (1967), in his field study of information gathering practices, defines scanning as the "systematization of information flowing into the organization to provide early warning of changing conditions."

Fahey and Narayanan (1986) portray scanning programs as a way for decision makers to understand changes taking place in their external environment. Scanning aids in forecasting change and brings expectations of change to bear on decision making.

Coates (1986) identifies the objectives of scanning as:

- Alerting management and staff to trends that are converging, diverging, speeding up, or slowing down
- Detecting scientific, technical, economic, social, and political interactions important to the organization
- Defining the threats, opportunities, or changes implied by those interactions
- Promoting a future-looking orientation in management and staff

Scanning can be described as a puzzle, where each piece of the puzzle is a category about which varying amounts of past, present, and future information is known. Some pieces are easier to understand than others; much is known about population growth because there are only a few variables: emigration, immigration, births, and deaths. Forecasts are easily available for the next 10 to 20 years. Other pieces of the puzzle (e.g., life styles and public attitudes) are less clear, but information is still available from traditional scanning sources: monographs, newsletters, journals, newspapers, and so on.

The issues management staff fits the pieces together to look for potential relationships. Pieces interact with one another, often in unexpected ways: population changes influence life-styles, which influence public attitudes, which influence voting, which leads to government programs, which can affect the economic well-being of organizations. The graying of America has influenced attitudes toward work and retirement. Political candidates supporting retirement reform receive support from those elderly who want to continue working, influencing elections, and, ultimately, producing legislation.

Defining Terms

The environment

Fahey and Narayanan (1986) describe several nested levels of environment. The task environment is a set of customers more or less specific to a particular organization. The industry environment includes all organizations associated with an industry. At the broadest level is the macroenvironment, where changes in the social, technological, economic, environmental, and political (STEEP) sectors affect businesses directly and indirectly.

The **social** sector includes demographics, lifestyles, and values. The **technological** sector concerns advances in pure and applied research, with their diffusion into every aspect of life and their generation of commercially viable technologies. The **economic** sector examines economic factors in the regional, national, and global society: e.g., GNP growth, disparity in income levels, and concentration of wealth. The **environmental** sector examines all other sectors from an environmental perspective, raising issues of energy conservation, recycling, ecosystem survival, hunger, and population growth. The **political** sector includes local, regional, national, and global politics (e.g., interest groups, regulatory agencies, and legislative bodies).

These sectors are interrelated — changes in one may lead to changes in another. A war in the Middle East causes the price of oil to rise, stimulating a recession. Technological developments in California enabling the production of low-cost, wind-generated electricity may be introduced worldwide, reducing the demand for fossil fuels and producing economic repercussions. Developments in the macroenvironment affect developments in the task and industrial environments, underscoring the necessity of scanning each environment to pick up early signs of change.

Scanning

Aguilar (1967) identifies four modes of scanning. *Undirected viewing* involves reading a variety of publications for no purpose other than to "be informed." *Conditioned viewing* is identical, save for assessing the information for its relevance to an organization. *Informal searching* seeks specific information in an unstructured way, in contrast to *formal searching,* which uses precise methodologies.

Passive and active scanning: Morrison, Renfro, and Boucher (1984) reduce these modes to passive and active scanning. Passive scanning is what most people do when they read journals or newspapers. For serious news coverage they tend to read the same sources: the local newspaper or a national newspaper like *The New*

York Times or *The Wall Street Journal.* As a consequence, the information cannot be used systematically as intelligence, and changes in the global environment that could affect the organization are missed. In order to broaden one's perspective and fight the tunnel vision inherent in everyone, active scanning is needed.

Active scanning selects sources spanning the STEEP sectors locally, regionally, nationally, and globally. It includes sources representing different dimensions of the same category (e.g., *The New Republic* and *The National Review* for the political sector at the national level).

Classifying scanning systems: Fahey, King, and Narayanan (1981) present a typology of scanning systems. Irregular systems are used on an ad hoc basis and tend to be crisis initiated: a planning committee needs specific information and conducts a scan for that purpose only. Periodic systems are used when a manager regularly updates a scan in preparation for a new planning cycle. Continuous systems inform the planning process systematically. Potentially relevant data are limited only by one's conception of what is relevant. The data are inherently scattered among a host of sources. Because early signals often appear in unexpected places, the scanning process must be broad and ongoing.

Monitoring

The terms" scanning" and "monitoring" are often used interchangeably; but as Fahey and Narayanan (1986) point out, monitoring follows scanning. Scanning detects signals of change. Once a signal is deemed important for the organization, monitoring begins.

Scanning identifies trends. The goal of monitoring is to assemble sufficient data to discern the past and future direction of trends.

Monitoring uses indicators of those trends as key words in a systematic search to obtain further information about them.

Setting up an Environmental Scanning Workshop

Establishing a continuous scanning system requires resources. At a minimum, it requires a professional and a support person to devote all their time to the enterprise, and a number of scanners who agree to review specific sources rigorously and systematically. One approach that has been successful in recruiting scanners is to offer a half- or full-day environmental scanning workshop.

Preparing an invitation

Invite managers from all divisions. Include members of the planning committee. Heterogeneity of backgrounds and perspectives guards against parochialism and will help one see into the future from others' points of view. The invitation should convey the idea that environmental scanning is essential for the future of the business. Stress that the information obtained will be used in the ongoing planning process.

Discuss a series of exercises wherein participants will identify and prioritize emerging issues, allowing them to bring their unique knowledge of the external environment to the discussion. The process of identifying trends should generate enthusiasm to be part of the scanning team. Appendix A includes strategic trends identified by petroleum executives in a workshop conducted by the authors.

Training scanners

In a full-day workshop, time can be spent training scanners for their task both in scanning and preparing abstracts. Stress that it is important to:

- Seek information about changes in the STEEP sectors on the local, regional, national, and global level. What change is taking place? What are the emerging trends? What data suggest the early stages of a trend? What events could affect the projections?
- Think holistically. Research on Alzheimer's disease may produce a drug to enhance memory capabilities. Research on solar or wind energy may portend significant savings in energy costs. The increasing availability of interactive videodisks and CD-ROMs may change how many training divisions function.
- Look for expert forecasts. Some experts say we are moving toward a sustainable world, based on energy efficiency, recycling, protecting ecosystems, and stabilizing world population. What are the implications for

your organization?... for the industry?

- Remember that matters that do not seem to affect the organization directly may be relevant.
- Remember that scanning is an art. There are no set rules for interpreting information correctly. Remember that every organization has a variety of stakeholders; try to view information from their points of view.

Information does not speak for itself. Skills, experience, and judgment are crucial to breathing life into them. The scanners' role is "to mold and shape material into a coherent whole; to present a vision; to help others imagine and reflect" (Neufeld, 1985, p. 44).

Writing abstracts

Ask: "If I had only a few minutes to describe this article to a friend, what would I say? What one idea most indicates change?" Whenever relevant, include statistical data. Limit the summary to no more than one-half page. Consider including a statement of implications for the organization, depending on what is wanted. Appendix B offers a sample abstract.

Other Components of a Strategic Trend Intelligence System

Establishing a Structure

The program need not be elaborate. A scanning committee should include at least one manager from each division to ensure that each area's concerns are represented and communications maintained.

The head of the issues management initiative should be chair of the committee. The chair assigns sources and collects copies of articles and abstracts. The committee should meet bimonthly or quarterly to sort and evaluate abstracts. The program may generate from 75 to 100 abstracts per quarter, depending on its scale.

Assigning Sources

Assigning materials for review provides confidence that most blips on the radar screen will be spotted. The committee should produce a list of reading materials and conferences to be reviewed. Try to assign scanners material they already read regularly. Ask for volunteers to read sources that are not read regularly by anyone. Spot check their progress. If there is a surplus of scanners, build in redundancy by having two or more people review the same source.

Selecting Trends to Monitor

Both the Issues Vulnerability Audit (IVA) described in Chapter 6, and internal management focus groups help select the material to be monitored. Focus groups work with senior managers to discover how they feel their ability to do their job has been affected by forces in the external environment. "When you forgot to drain the swamp, which of the alligators' bites hurt the worst?" It is the thoughtful comments of line managers about these forces that help establish a meaningful taxonomy.

Conducting a Committee Meeting

A committee meeting should be held every two-to-three months to review material that has been amassed during that period. To prepare for the meeting, the chair should sort abstracts by subject area (e.g., office automation goes in one pile; employee compensation goes in another pile; miscellaneous topics go in a third).

Each committee member is assigned a packet of abstracts to review in detail. All members read all of the abstracts but come to the meeting prepared to discuss trends and issues from the abstracts in their set, examining how they relate to trends identified previously.

An alternative is for each member to review all of the abstracts and come to the meeting prepared to sort them into three categories: winners, losers, and toss-ups. Regardless of the format used, the meeting will last from two-to-four hours, including time for each person to speak and time for an open discussion. The outcome should be a brief summary of 15 or so trends, imminent events, and emerging issues to present to the steering committee.

Developing a Scanning Taxonomy

The trends identified in the initial planning and in the scanning workshop may be used to develop the beginnings of a taxonomy, so that every item resulting from scanning has a logical place to be classified. There are two objectives: to provide a comprehensive set of categories, and to provide a numbering method for each piece of information collected. Appendix C is an example of a taxonomy developed at Sears. The Sears taxonomy can be modified. Or, one may prefer to develop a taxonomy as one goes, using key words from the abstracts as categories. The important thing is to tailor the taxonomy to the peculiarities of the organization.

Publishing a Newsletter

A scanning newsletter can bring important trends to the attention of all members of the organization and provide recognition for the efforts of scanners. Trends identified between committee meetings should be included.

This newsletter could stand alone or be inserted in another. The issues manager may want to design a logo, use distinctive paper, or experiment with boxes labeled "Wild Speculations," "Wild Cards," or "Left Field."

Broadly solicit comments and contributions. Make the format and content readable.

Case in point: Repetitive Stress Injuries

The debate over repetitive stress injuries (RSI) is heating up. It is being fueled by the growing number of lawsuits (at least 3000 high-stakes suits) filed against equipment makers alleging unsafe design. In 1993 over 1,200 newspaper and magazine articles covered the RSI issue. Dozens of these articles referred to RSI as the next great epidemic. This media attention just didn't appear over-night. Equipment manufacturers monitoring this issue should have assessed its potential impact years ago. The major defendants in this issue appear to be

IBM, AT&T and Eastman Kodak Co. They could have used anticipatory management techniques, to either remedy the issue or at least keep it from becoming debated and judged in the press. Some companies, including Sara Lee Corporation's bakeries and Harley-Davidson, have reported major improvements after active involvement in the issue. Their actions are not unlike United Airlines involvement in the VDT issue. As with other issues such as video display terminals (VDTs), and electro-magnetic fields (EMFs), there is a paucity of scientific information on the RSI issue at this time. That lack of scientific information has not stopped the courts from making awards or the regulators from doing their thing. OSHA has said it will propose ergonomic requirements in the fall of 1994. The question of how long it will take to have a new legal theory prevail is not known, but plaintiff's lawyers argue that "law can't wait on science."

General Robert E. Wood, one of the chief engineers of the Panama Canal, passed his leisure time scanning statistical abstracts from the Bureau of Labor Statistics. He noticed population trends indicating a movement from central cities to the suburbs. Upon leaving the military he became chairman at Sears, Roebuck & Co., whose business at the time was almost exclusively in catalog sales. Wood continued to monitor the population shifts, using the information to launch the greatest expansion in the history of retailing, building some stores in the middle of cow pastures.

The lesson was well learned. Monitoring trends in the automobile industry enabled Sears to spot the need for affordable automobile insurance and launch one of the most successful insurance companies in the industry: Allstate.

Sources for Scanning

Literature

The primary criterion for selecting literature is diversity: newspapers, magazines, dissertations, journals, TV and radio programs, conferences, and knowledgeable individuals should be included.

Sources are not lacking. *Future Survey Annual* 1988-89 lists 454 futures-related periodicals, including 46 in international economics and development, 45 in environmental resources and energy, and 31 in health and human services. Many organizations have publicly available scans. The World Future Society (7910 Woodmont Avenue, Suite 450, Bethesda MD 20814) publishes *Future Survey,* a monthly collection of book, article, and report abstracts. The Global Network (1101 30th St. NW, Suite 130, Washington DC 20007) publishes *John Naisbitt's Trend Letter.* Kiplinger Washington Editors (1729 H St. NW, Washington DC 20006) publishes the *Kiplinger Washington Letter.* The authors personally have prepared two scans, Global FutureScan 2000 and FutureScan 2000, which are updated periodically. Suggested American newspapers include *The New York Times,* the *Washington Post, The Wall Street Journal,* the *Miami Herald,* the *Chicago Tribune,* the *Los Angeles Times,* and *The Christian*

Science Monitor. Three excellent British newspapers are *The Times, The Independent,* and *The Guardian.* Suggested magazines include *Vital Speeches of the Day, Across the Board, Time, Newsweek, U.S. News and World Report, Futures, The Forum for Applied Research and Public Policy, World Monitor, Atlantic, The Nation, Ms, Utné Reader,* and *The Futurist.*

To ensure that scanning is adequate, one must identify sources for each STEEP category at each level, from local through global. A comprehensive list should include the following:

Social Literature: In the U.S., include *American Demographics, Public Opinion* and publications from the Census Bureau, other governmental agencies, university sociology departments, and population study centers. National Technical and Information Services and the Department of Labor offer demographic studies. The National Center for Health Statistics provides data on such areas as fertility and life expectancy. The U.S. League of Savings Associations studies home-buyer demographics, and the American Council of Life Insurance also conducts demographic studies. The United Nations and the Organization for Economic and Cooperative Development are good sources of reports. In the U.K., see *New Society* and publications from the Department of Trade and Industry for general demographics, and the Department of Health and Social Services for fertility and life expectancy. The Building Societies Association has data on home-buyer demographics.

Technological Literature: Sources you may wish to review include:
Technological Review, Datamation, BYTE, Computer World, Discover, InfoWorld, Science, Scientific American, The Whole Earth Review, Nature, New Scientist, and *Proceedings of the National Academy of Sciences.*

Economic Literature: Check *Business Week, The Economist, Fortune, Forbes, Money, Inc., The Monthly Labor Review, The Financial Times,* and publications from the Department of Commerce's Bureau of Economic Analysis and the departments of Labor, Energy, and Treasury. State and local agencies provide comparable regional data. In the U.K., the BBC's *Money Programme* presents a weekly review of national and international economic trends and events. Lloyds Bank produces regular reports on different nations.

Environmental Literature: For environmental trends, see *Ecodecision* (Royal Society of Canada, 276 Rue Saint-Jacque Oest, Bureau 924, Montreal H24 IN3 Canada), *Environment* (Heldres Publications, 4000 Albermarle St. NW, Washington DC 20016) and publications of the Global Tomorrow Coalition (1325 G St. NW, Suite 915, Washington DC 20005-3140), Worldwatch Institute (1776 Massachusetts Ave. NW, Washington DC 20036), Island Press (1718 Connecticut Ave. NW, Washington DC 20009), The Audubon Society, and the Sierra Club. In Europe, Friends of the Earth (U.K.) issues periodic reports, and the German Development

Agency publishes an English-language journal, *Development and Cooperation.*

Political Literature: *New Republic, The National Review, The National Journal, In These Times, Mother Jones, Federal Register, Congressional Quarterly, Weekly Report,* and *The Digest of Public General Bills.* In the U.K., reference *New Statesman* and *Harsard.* Other sources include public opinion leaders and social critics, think tanks (e.g., the Hudson Institute, the Institute for the Future, the Brookings Institute, and the American Enterprise Institute), and governmental documents (e.g., transcripts of hearings, proposed legislation). State legislatures (National Conference of State Legislatures, Marketing Department, 1560 Broadway Suite 700, Denver CO 80202) offers a periodic summary of pending legislation. One's own network of friends and colleagues is also useful.

Electronic databases

A variety of electronic databases is available on a subscription basis from ABI Inform, Educational Resources Information Center (ERIC), Public Affairs Information Service (PAIS), Dialogue, Bibliographic Retrieval Service (BRS), and others. They are particularly amenable to monitoring.

Bibliographic databases can be used to store information, facilitating review and update of data. An electronic filing system aids development of relationships with other organizations. Packages include *Pro-Cite* from Personal

Bibliographic Software, which has standard forms for data entry, authority lists for standardizing entries, and a search facility using propositional logic. It is available both in Macintosh and MS-DOS formats. Personal Bibliographic Software offers two complementary programs, *Pro-Search* and *Bibliolinks,* for retrieving information from databases to transfer into an appropriate *Pro-Cite* form. It is also possible to use a standard database program like *dBase IV* or *Oracle.*

Pitfalls to Avoid in Establishing and Using a Strategic Trend Intelligence System

In a service and information economy, information is the principal source of power and recognition. Although the establishment of a strategic trend intelligence system within an organization is highly desirable, there are caveats.

I am new and smarter-than-you syndrome

Many times the skills needed to operate a scanning unit are very broad.These skills do not exist within the organization, and someone has to be hired from outside. The newcomers may feel a need to demonstrate their expertise. They define the purpose of their existence as educating the uninformed, spelling out in detail the formal, analytical techniques of their work. Managers with years of experience assume they know everything they need to about their job and company. They view trend assessment as a profit drain — the CEO's latest whim — and offer little support. The scanning unit becomes isolated from day-to-day business. The issues management group attempts to justify its existence by sending out lengthy academic reports on complex trends that managers have little or no interest in and no time to read.

Damned if you do . . .

The unit is placed at the top corporate level, feeding information only to senior staff or commenting on the feasibility of plans that are in their final stages. The unit is well out of the mainstream. If its members agree with what they are asked to comment on, they are seen as redundant. If they disagree, regardless of the quality of their input, senior managers call them "nay-sayers." Either way, they lose.

No quid pro quo

The unit's ability to function depends on its ability to understand what is happening at the line manager level. Yet, there are no incentives for managers to provide information because they see no quid pro quo. (What's in it for me?)

Chicken Little complex

In a last-ditch effort to make its presence known, the unit becomes a Chicken Little, writing memos to senior staffers about impending chaos. Realistically, most trends are not enough to make the sky fall. The newly appointed issues manager should watch out for these and other pitfalls. Failure to do so will often result in the unit being shut down and the manager seeking a new job as a consultant. The irony is that as an outside consultant, the person may end up serving the exact same function for the company at a much higher reward level.

Summary

Building a strategic trend intelligence system is a relatively inexpensive way to address emerging issues quickly. Through participating in the scanning process, senior managers develop a shared understanding of issues and the changing environment of the organization. The scanning process facilitates team building, focuses attention on the long-term future, and insures that the intelligence gathered has support from top management. Scanning can be further developed to understand the evolution of the issue life cycle, as we shall see in the next chapter.

CHAPTER FIVE

Power Tool Number Three

The Issue Life Cycle

Special interest groups are more numerous, more sophisticated, and better funded than ever before. They listen to their constituents more closely. Meanwhile, business sits back and relies on the outmoded and occasionally embarrassing practice of lobbying on an issue after others have set the agenda.

Too often, business and industry have ignored issues until it is only possible to reduce the negative consequences of proposed legislation. As a result, critics charge that business is always against new legislation. In fact, business and industry frequently are "reactive," since an issue may have developed for months, even years, with little or no business input prior to the legislative phase.

— National Association of Manufacturers, 1992.

When businesses do not engage in anticipatory planning, their ability to help define an issue, set the agenda, and establish the limits of the issue is limited. An issue ignored is a crisis invited.

Special interest groups concentrate their efforts on newspapers like *The New York Times* and the *Washington Post.* When stories appear in these papers, it is almost certain that key people in Washington have been and will be discussing them.

Generally, it will not be the first time the information has been "kited." Usually, the story has run the gamut of the non-mainstream press, and has been picked up by a larger publication, such as the *The Economist.* When a story hits the *New York Times* or the *Washington Post,* it has matured to the point where influencing it is nearly impossible. In principle, the media does not tell its audience what to think; in practice, it does say what they should be thinking about.

When it comes to setting the public agenda, business has been notoriously slow and even reluctant to become involved. Joseph Nolan (1985) points out that:

Business people have been slow to recognize the importance of shaping issues because they perceive it as an academic exercise. When an issue is of concern to society, business says, whether through arrogance or ignorance, "That's interesting, but what has it got to do with making widgets (flying airplanes, making hamburgers, etc.)?..."

Business people are uncomfortable dealing with vague concepts. Without an easily recognizable path to the bottom line that can be seen clearly by everyone, an issue, trend or driving force will be ignored.

Business has trouble agreeing on what issues to put on the agenda. The only time business is unified is when it is the target of a special interest group or government agency. Big business often finds itself at odds with small business; free traders vie with protectionists; and capital intensive businesses are at odds with labor intensive ones.

Business has little choice but to get involved in public issues. Groups with anticipatory skills have a growing advantage when confronting the wide range of issues within the purview of government and special interest groups.

Outmoded lobbying techniques and overrated Political Action Committee (PAC) dollars are not enough to compete in the agenda-setting of the '90s. While these strategies may still get an audience with a legislator, without well-considered positions and white papers, numbers, and details to support its arguments, business will be out-thought by its opponents.

The Tyranny of the Small Majority

Unless business wishes to continue losing the battle with special interests by always playing the role of nay-sayer, it will have to realize that the "seagull theory" is an ineffective strategy in the long run.

Seagull Theory of Issues Involvement

The seagull is a notorious oceanfront bird that every once in a while deposits its well-digested meal on those below. When applied to business, the seagull's counterpart is the CEO who flies in on the corporate jet, deposits some well-digested ideas from his or her perspective on Capitol Hill (i.e., testifies on a bill), and flies away, confident the payload has hit its target and something will be done.

Case in Point: The Alar Incident

According to Cynthia Crossen in her book *Tainted Truth,* there may never be a definitive answer to the question of whether the agricultural chemical daminozide, known as Alar, causes cancer in humans. But, she points out, the decision has been made to ban the use of Alar.

Alar had been sprayed on apples to prolong shelflife since the '60s. However, in 1980, evidence began to appear that convinced regulators that Alar violated the Delaney Amendment. Alar was found to cause tumors in laboratory animals.

By 1989, without an official government ban in place, only 5-40 percent of the apples grown in the U.S. were sprayed with Alar.

In 1989, the Natural Resources Defense Council (NRDC), an environmental advocacy group, was able to strike a decisive blow with a risk assessment study titled, *Intolerable Risk: Pesticides in our Children's Food.* This white paper came after years of putting pressure on the regulators to ban Alar. With the help of an aggressive media campaign, which included the actress Meryl Streep as spokesperson, the campaign took on the proportions of a natural disaster.

After the fact, the apple industry hired a public relations firm. Three federal agencies—the Environmental Protection Agency (EPA), the Food and Drug Administration (FDA), and the Department of Agriculture—stated they believed Alar to be safe. This reaction came too late to control the damage. In June of 1989, Uniroyal, the maker of Alar, withdrew it from the market.

The lesson here is, a special interest group with a very narrow agenda can upset a whole industry with less than objective truth and a well-orchestrated campaign, if that industry is not prepared. Being prepared comes from anticipatory management, not reactive behavior.

The Issue Life Cycle

In many cases, special interest groups direct their efforts toward the staffers who draft the legislation on which Congress votes. They arrive with independently prepared, well-researched papers, having learned long ago that to influence legislation, one must anticipate it and act accordingly.

To anticipate emerging issues that drive legislation, it is important first to understand a central concept in anticipatory management. That is, the stages of an issue conform to a life cycle that respond to shifts in the external environment (Starling, 1980).

Wilson (1982) describes the issue life-cycle in four phases: Societal expectations, policy agenda, formalization, and social control.

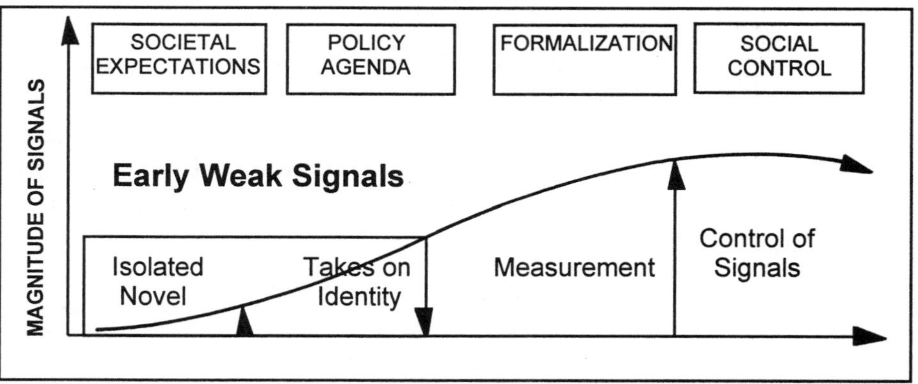

Figure 5.1 Life cycle of an issue.

Phase 1- Societal expectations

Societal expectations change in ways that at first are subtle, often imperceptible, to even the most careful observer. It takes someone to articulate them in a way that raises societal awareness, a function typically fulfilled by a number of different players. Molitor (1975) believes that expectation shifts are encouraged by a number of people:

- Innovators
- Leading experts
- Public-spirited crusaders
- "Think tank" scholars
- Government-sponsored researchers
- Academics
- "Invisible college" members
- Public policy researchers (e.g., Brookings scholars)
- Authors
- Issue popularizers (book reviewers, cabbies, hair stylists)

A classic example of awareness-raising occurred with Rachel Carson's 1963 publication of *Silent Spring,* a devastating account of how we are destroying our environment. Her warnings about the use of DDT helped avert an ecological disaster.

Recent shifts in U.S. policy demonstrate the power of expectations. Policy changes on the environment, civil rights, consumer rights, product safety, workplace hazards, and pesticides resulted from social consensus. Almost no major policy innovations are enacted at the federal level that are not preceded by years of national discussion.

It is at the societal expectation phase that organizations should consider becoming involved. In the expectations phase, organizations are often established in the demand for "something to be done." The issues are named "fair credit," "environmental protection," "product safety". Names provide substance to the issue in the minds of the public. The growth in interest groups around an issue, measured by the number of people, organizations, or resources committed — tends to be exponential, forcing serious consideration of the issue by public policy makers.

Phase 2 - Policy agenda

The articulation of an issue does not automatically lead to a policy agenda — a set of items given active consideration. Sufficient societal concerns will eventually reach attentive and eager lawmakers who see an opportunity to bring the concerns of their constituents to a policy level. That consideration may appear in a presidential inaugural speech, the State of the Union address, or a governor's "State of the State" address.

At this stage in the life cycle, the issue is being dealt with at the local, state, or federal level. Specific remedies to address the issue are being debated. Opportunities for intervention are limited to modifying, rephrasing, or opposing the content of the initiative.

Phase 3 - Formalization

Once an issue reaches the agenda level, the process of formalizing a set of "fix it" rules can begin. The final result is legislative action which can be enforced through the courts.

At this stage of the issue life cycle, the policies are formalized and implementation has begun. Some government agency is assigned to monitor compliance with the initiative. Options available to the affected industry are limited to "weeping, wailing and gnashing of teeth," questioning of enforcement techniques, and attempts to make the rules easier to live with.

Phase 4 - Social control

The degree of success in issue resolution depends on enforcement by the responsible agencies, and compliance by the businesses affected. Public attention tends to decline, then level off. In the meantime, compliance can be costly, as will be demonstrated by the following discussion.

A Difficult Lesson to Learn

Although Wilson modeled the life cycle of issues in 1982, many business leaders still do not fully understand its relevance to their organizations. Managers fail to recognize rising societal expectations out of complacency or arrogance. In many cases, the wave of social change is not detected until it reaches the social control phase and penalties are enforced. Figure 5.2 shows the typical behaviors managers exhibit through the phases of the issue life cycle.

Much like the people in Kubler-Ross' model of responses to death and dying, managers in the second phase resort to denial, saying things like, "no one would be dumb enough to pass such a law," or "they wouldn't dare do something like that." When an issue reaches Phase 3, and a bill is ready for signatures, the response is "let's

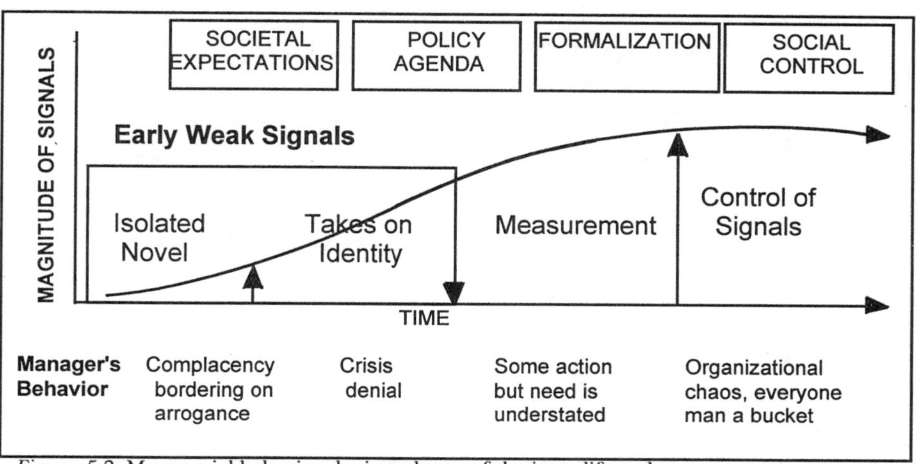

Figure 5.2 Managerial behavior during phases of the issue life cycle.

make some phone calls," or "send our folks to Washington to call in some chits."

Issues of the '70s

A review of several issues from the '70s shows how social expectations moved to the policy agenda, inspired legislation, and led to social control.

Environmental protection

Although Rachel Carson's book did not itself start the environmental revolution, it raised awareness about questionable industrial practices. The public became concerned about the misuse of pesticides and subsequent damage to watersheds, moving presidential candidate Eugene McCarthy to address environmental issues in his platform. The Clean Air Act and Clean Water Act, passed in 1970 and 1972 respectively, were used in 1976 to assess a $7 million penalty against the General Electric Co.

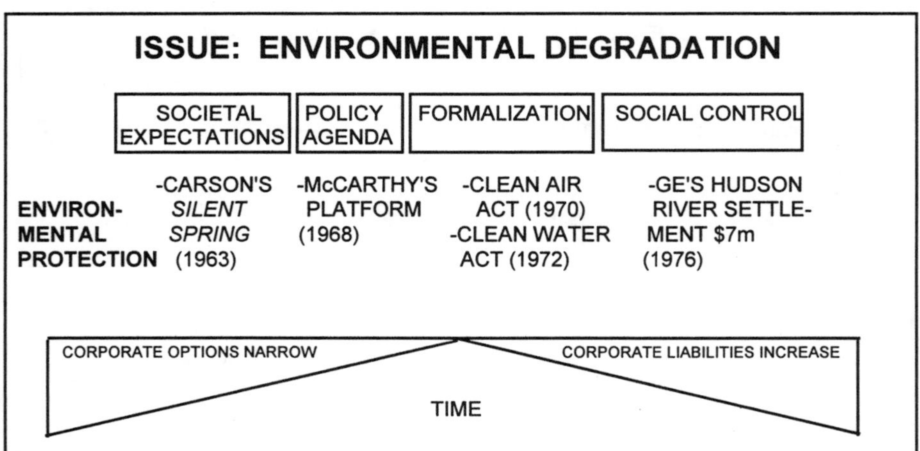

Figure 5.3 Issue emerges from environmental degradation to environmental protection.

for contamination to the Hudson River.

Unfair Employment Practices

The Civil Rights Act of 1964 was a culmination of events (see Figure 5.4). The 1954 decision in *Brown v. the Board of Education* and the 1963 publication of Betty Friedan's *The Feminine Mystique* raised societal expectations for ethnic and gender equality.

Lyndon Johnson made equal rights a major part of his 1964 platform. In a June 1965 speech to the graduating class of Howard University, he stated:

> *It is not enough to open the gates of opportunity. All our citizens must have the ability to walk through those gates.... This is the next and the more profound stage of the battle for civil rights. We seek not just freedom, but opportunity.*

The Equal Pay Act of 1963 made it illegal to pay women less than men for substantially the same work.

Johnson issued Executive orders 11246 and 11375, which require companies of 50 or more employees holding federal contracts over a certain dollar amount to implement a written affirmative-action plan.

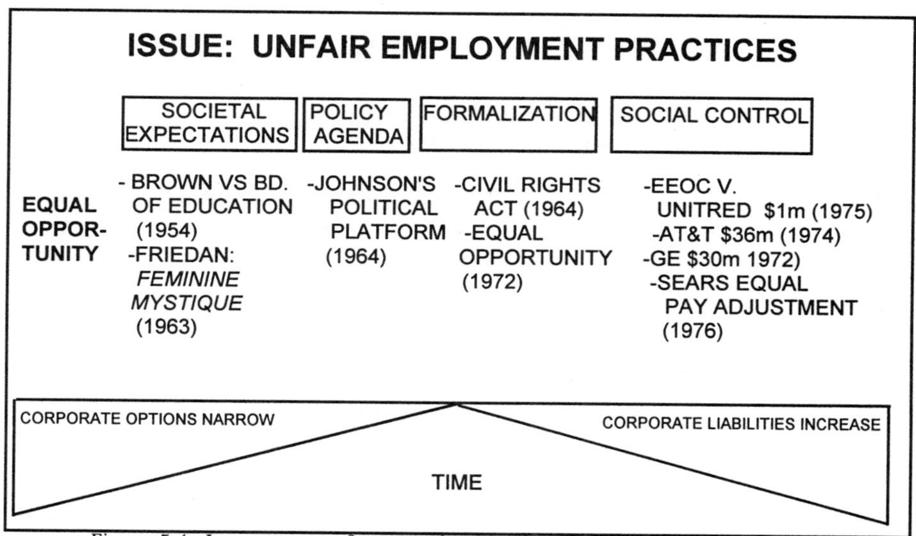

Figure 5.4 Issue emerges from employment practices to become equal opportunity.

Although most of these actions occurred in the early '60s, they were largely ignored by business through the early '70s. In 1973, under heavy federal pressure, AT&T agreed to give women and minority employees wage increases amounting to $36 million in the first year. The company paid another $15 million to satisfy job discrimination claims.

General Electric paid $30 million in 1972 for failure to adhere to the new Equal Employment Opportunity Commission (EEOC) guidelines.

In 1976, Sears, Roebuck and Co. was forced to pay female employees $50 million in an equal pay adjustment as a result of policies that violated the Equal Pay Act. Company CEO Arthur Wood, concerned that such a violation could go unnoticed for so long, put in place the country's first strategic issues management program.

Consumer product safety

In 1972, Congress passed the Consumer Product Safety Act, creating a Consumer Product Safety Commission to remove "unreasonable risk" from consumer products. As early as 1964, consumer advocate Ralph Nader raised awareness about product design with his campaign against the Corvair automobile. Shortly thereafter Thalidomide, a muscle relaxant for pregnant women, resulted in widespread birth defects, raising product safety to the policy agenda and legislative stages.

As late as 1976, Firestone Tire & Rubber marketed a tire they knew to be defective. Two years later, the government accused Firestone of selling defective tires. According to federal authorities, the 500 series of radials was prone to blow outs, tread separation, and other deformities. It was also the target of numerous consumer complaints. The tires were implicated in hundreds of accidents and at least 34 deaths. Public relations blitzes and attempts to

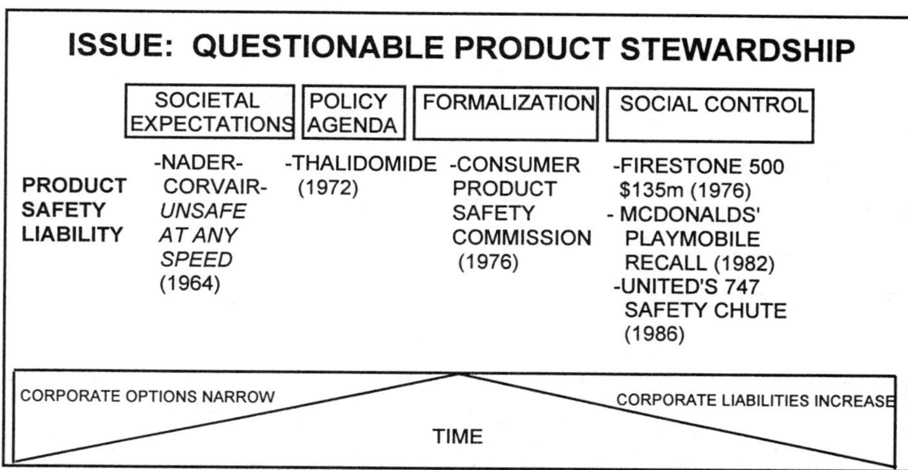

Figure 5.5 Issue emerges from questionable product stewardship to become product safety liability.

thwart the investigation only irritated consumers. In the end, $135 million in liability damages was assessed against the company.

On the other hand

United Airlines uncovered minor problems with the safety slides on its fleet of Boeing 747 aircraft. Although no problem existed as far as regulators (the Federal Aviation Administration and the Department of Transportation) were concerned, United anticipated the problem and systematically repaired the 747s with little disruption to business and without being told to do so. Had United waited, an inspector might have grounded the fleet, resulting in substantial revenue loss and widespread customer dissatisfaction.

Early warning signals are available for a company that wishes to manage issues rather than be managed by them. Those companies that choose to ignore signals get a rude awakening.

Those companies that anticipate and respond to signals neatly sidestep catastrophe.

Using the Life Cycle of Issues in Anticipatory Management

Figure 5.6 shows how the flow of corporate anticipatory management parallels the flow of the issue life cycle. Early signals of rising societal expectations should lead to managerial considerations, organizational actions, and well considered policies. The following examples in

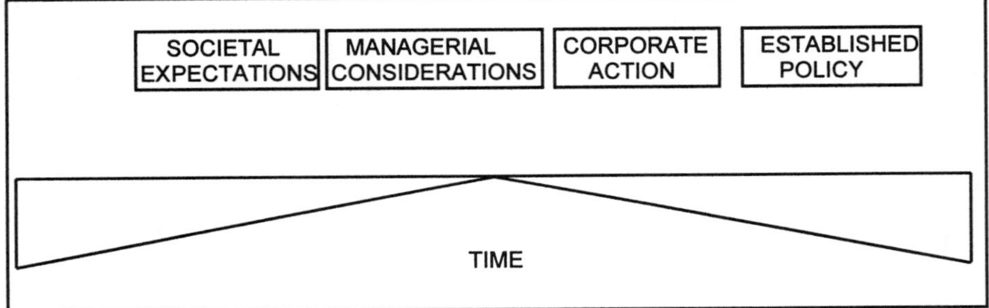

Figure 5.6 Corporate involvement in the issue life cycle.

the airline and food industries illustrate how anticipatory management actions affect the issue life cycle.

Video display terminals (VDTs)

Although concern over VDTs has been around for a number of years and referred to by many names, it has not to date resulted in unreasonable regulation. This is due, in large measure, to sound anticipatory management techniques by United Airlines and other companies taken early in the issue's life cycle. Although first discussed in the '60s, when such terms as "ergonomics" were yet to be coined, health risks from VDTs gained new attention in the early '80s when the Clerical Workers Union, The Newspaper Guild, and the National Organization for Women used them to try to raise waning membership. Their claims centered on possible miscarriages from radiation emission and behavioral problems due to stress.

Through United Airlines' anticipatory management function, the VDT issue was brought to the attention of senior management, analyzed, and transformed into a plan of action. Reservation office VDT ergonomics were inspected with regard to lighting, positioning, temperature, and glare, and managers were informed of union concerns. Reservation offices were gradually renovated under the direction of an ergonomic architect.

United spearheaded a coalition building effort. Analysis revealed that manufacturers and users could be on opposite sides of the debate. Any regulation requiring unnecessary enhancement to the equipment would be born by the user and benefit the manufacturer.

The coalition attempted to bring together users, especially from the insurance and banking industries. Much to the chagrin of United's issue manager, the associations of both industries had neither heard of, nor were concerned about the issue. It took some persuading for them to inform their members of the costs and restrictions that could result if the debate went against them. The associations of all three industries established the Coalition for Office Technology. One of the coalition's proactive tactics was to write well-considered testimony for the public affairs representatives to deliver in Washington and various state capitals.

United then developed policies vis-a-vis the use and deployment of VDTs within the company. Figures 5.7 and 5.8 compare the life cycle of this issue with industry anticipatory management actions.

Food industry under siege

The life cycle of the food industry's product stewardship issue began with societal concerns about drugs in milk, salmonella in chicken, Alar on apples, and unsanitary handling of beef that lead to media attention and heightened societal awareness.

The issue progressed to the policy agenda phase when the actions of public interest groups brought it to the attention of the Food and Drug Administration and the Department of Agriculture. At this writing, the last two phases in the life cycle (legislative requirements and social control) have not been determined, although proposals for meat inspection and other safety measures are mounting. The ball is in the food industry's court.

As figure 5.10 shows, in terms of the anticipatory management model, the industry has begun to respond. They have reviewed present methods, processes, and policies as they relate to cleanliness and sanitation. Their current actions include adding microbiologists to establish sanitation techniques, initiating computer-assisted cleaning controls, designing and

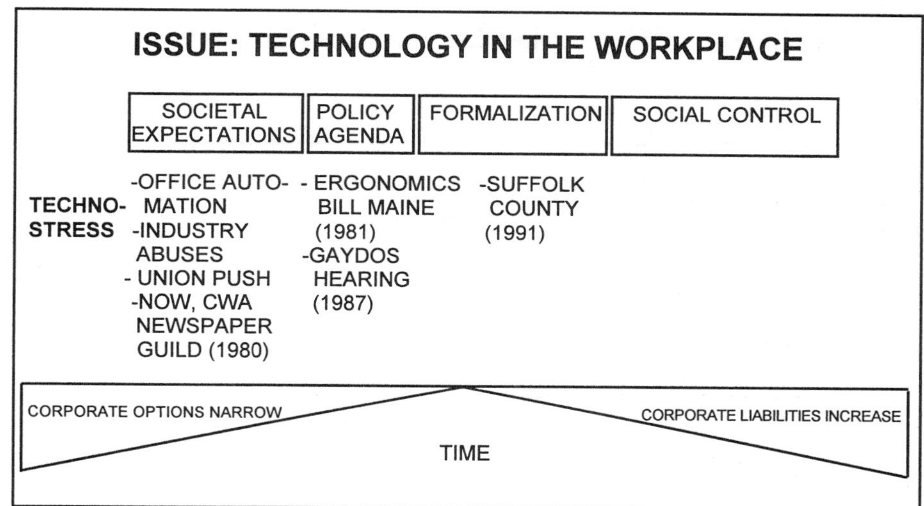

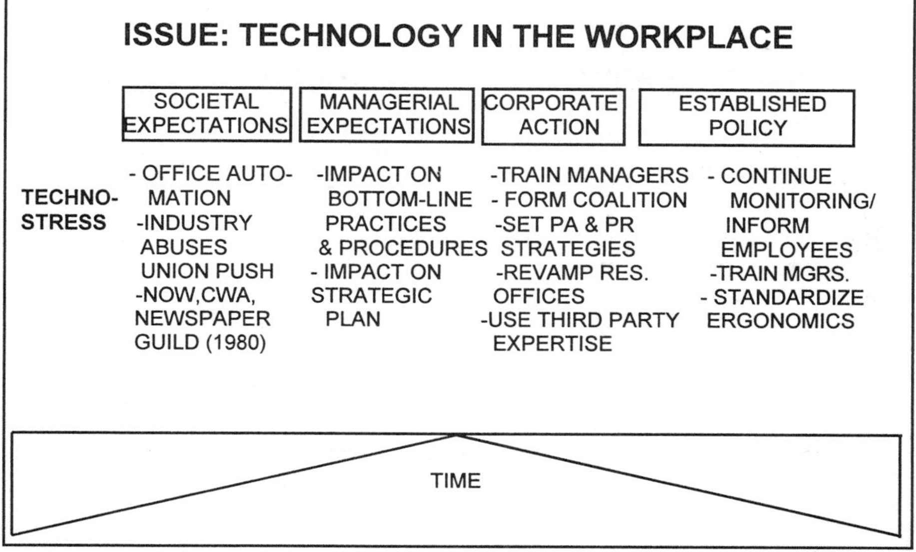

Figure 5.8 Corporate involvement in the issue life cycle.

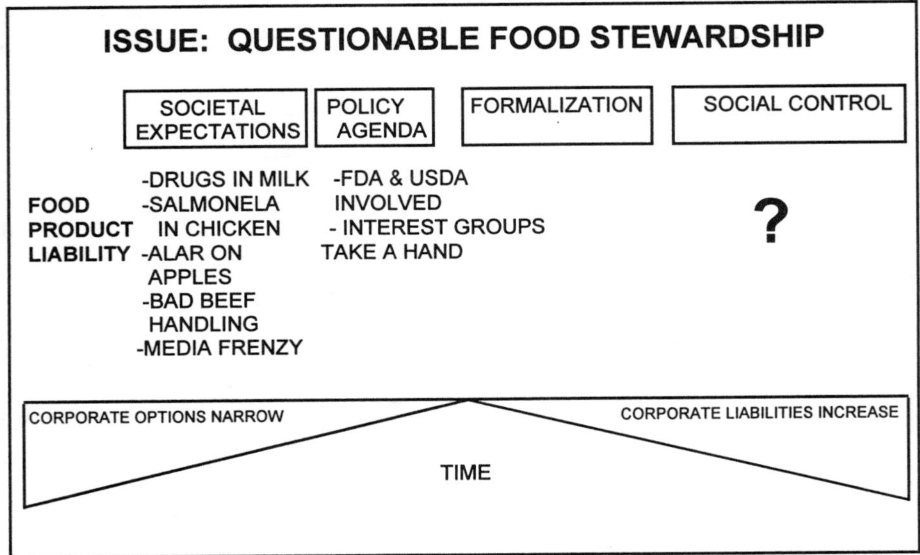

Figure 5.9 Issue emerging from questionable food handling.

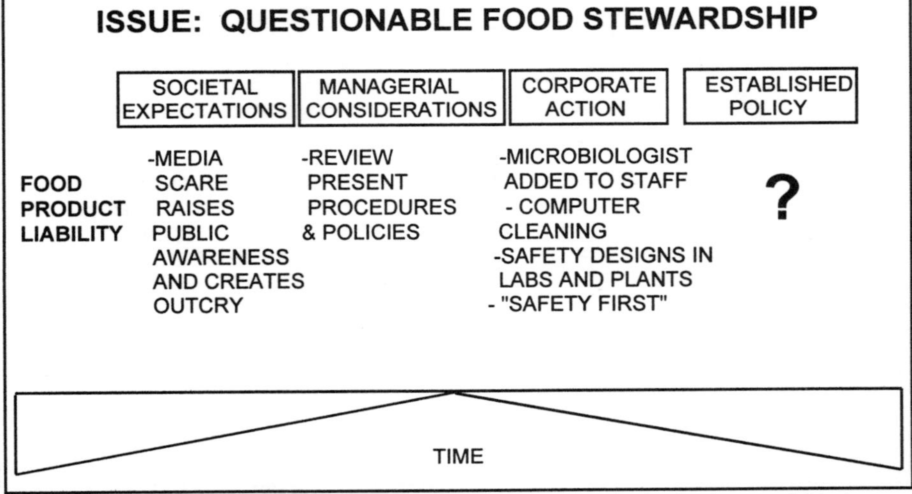

Figure 5.10 Corporate involvement in the food stewardship issue.

incorporating safety methods into food handling procedures, and setting up laboratories in some food handling plants for inspection and control. "Safety first" has become the order of the day.

"Infoductiveness"

A phenomenon we have termed "infoductiveness" has shortened the length of time from the societal expectations to the control stage dramatically. Information reaches a larger, more sophisticated audience in a shorter period of time. Infoductiveness has shortened the time available for corporations to get their acts together. The penalties that are being imposed are of historic proportions.

As issues move along the time line suggested by Wilson, the warning signals grow in intensity. The opportunity for corporate intervention lessens, and the pressure of fiscal liabilities increases.

Summary

Issues are central to the planning process. Thinking of the life cycle of issues in just the context of public policy limits the ability of managers to anticipate the broad range of strategic issues that might impact the organization's performance. Consequently, an effective anticipatory management program incorporates much more than is found in many planning efforts.

Too often strengths, weaknesses, opportunities, and threats are treated as if they exist only at the beginning of the planning cycle, captured in a snapshot. Anticipatory management uses ongoing scanning and monitoring to provide a motion picture of the external environment that can be used to assess marketing initiatives, the competition's initiatives, technological development, and human resource concerns.

Our argument rests on the belief that the role of the corporation has changed from merely an economic institution that exists to make profits for the shareholder, to a sociopolitical entity that must balance the economic realities with societal expectations. Therefore, relationships within the corporation must change as well. Rather than making the departmental foxholes deeper, we must channel between them to make them more interconnected than ever before. As the country moves further toward an information-driven economy, the need for new models becomes clear.

The playing field is different. It is bigger; and our structures, relationships, laws, and social policies put us at the far end of that field. The techniques of anticipatory management can overcome some of the difficulties. We must not constrain its application by defining it too narrowly. The strength of anticipatory management lies in its analytical techniques and its ability to look ahead.

CHAPTER SIX

Power Tool Number Four

The Issues Vulnerability Audit

Many start-up issues management programs have fallen prey to the child's theory of the hammer. The child's theory of the hammer holds that when a child is given a hammer, everything starts to look like a nail. When given the responsibility to manage issues, everything begins to look like an issue.

The issues vulnerability audit (IVA), originally developed as vulnerability analysis by SRI International in 1977, reveals subtle, overlooked opportunities or threats that fall outside the normal sphere of organizational activity. It lends itself to a kind of strategic thinking that forces managers to view trends through the eyes of friendly and hostile stakeholders before the trends go critical.

Vulnerability audits are based on four assumptions about organizations:

- They exist to serve some societal need;
- They rely on support from their external world;
- They are vulnerable to changes in that external world; and
- They are supported by many critical elements.

Organizations are like ocean oil rigs whose supports go deep into the sea to rest on the bedrock. An organization's supports include the needs it meets, the resources it relies on, and the customers it serves. Those supports also include the organization's cost stability, logos, technologies, and integrity.

The issues vulnerability audit reviews these supports from the perspective of current strengths. The supports are turned into questions: What needs and desires does the organization meet? On what resources does it rely? What cost advantages are available? What special abilities does the organization have? What technologies underpin it?

To really grasp a sense of how vulnerable the organization might be to outside forces that are less than friendly or even hostile, the vulnerability audit then examines the supports' vulnerability to removal, alteration, or substantial disruption. Vulnerabilities may result from competitive forces, governmental intervention, special interest group initiatives, scientific discoveries, media disclosures, and so on.

Conducting an Audit

The audit should be conducted by a relatively small team (12 to 24 members) of senior leaders from across the organization, each representing a major functional area. It is important that senior leaders be directly involved, because they can offer quality input, and because the results could lead to extensive reorganization or major changes in direction.

It is desirable to have an off-site location for a day or two to conduct the audit. The group should be divided into teams of six-to-eight members. Each team will answer the above questions for each support. It may be desirable to use a two-part exercise: consider first the strengths of each category; then have each team act in an adversarial role to respond to the vulnerability questions. This requires a good deal of imagination. Have participants imagine that they are endowed with unlimited power to see into the next decade and destroy the supports.

It may be helpful to begin the audit with one of the environmental scans mentioned in Chapter 7. Having a sense of the driving forces for change in the social, technological, economic, environmental, and political arenas provides the managers with an understanding of the scope of forces of change as well as an ability to put the audit in the context of the future.

Discovering Strategic Organizational Supports

The first step is to identify as many supports as possible on which the organization depends. A support can be tangible (a physical resource) or intangible (legislation, or social values that make a product desirable).

Needs and wants served by an organization

These change. The buggy whip served to motivate horses, a strength for buggy whip makers. With the advent of a new technology — the horseless carriage — the need for buggy whips declined as horses were no longer relied on for work and transportation.

A relevant *strength* question is: What customer needs and wants does the organization satisfy?

Relevant *vulnerability* questions include: Could a need be served another way by some other organization? Could the need for a product or service disappear? Under what circumstances?

Resources and Assets

Resources and assets include people, capital, energy, raw material, facilities, equipment, postal services, telephone systems, and fax systems, distribution systems, and cooperative arrangements with other organizations.

A relevant *strength* question would be: What additional uses might the organization find for its resources?

Relevant *vulnerability* questions include: What happens if a resource is no longer available? Are there substitutes? How much would they cost? How quickly could they be obtained? Are we demonstrating good stewardship in the use of our resources?

It is important to include the entire range of materials and services and to ask what would happen if the organization no longer had access to any of them (e.g., what would happen if the power station had a fire?).

Customer base

Organizations exist by their ability to serve customers, who often are a narrowly specialized group: Gucci caters to a high-income customer base, while Sears, Wal-Mart, and K-Mart have a low- to middle-income base.

Relevant *strength* questions include: What is our present customer base? How can we expand our customer base?

Relevant *vulnerability* questions would be: How might our customer base shift? (For example, the 1986 tax reform imposed a penalty on luxury items over a certain dollar amount, limiting the sale of yachts, luxury automobiles, and exotic furs.) How might we lose customers to the competition? Are there demographic shifts of which we should be aware? The massive decline in the teenage population from the late '70s to the late '80s severely affected organizations employing or marketing to that group. What is the possibility that customers will provide the services for themselves?

Cost stability relative to the competition

Organizations seek to gain cost advantages over the competition through volume, vertical integration, or special supplier relationships.

The key *strength* questions include: How can we preserve our cost stability? Is it possible to extend the advantages we have to other areas?

The key *vulnerability* questions would be: Is it possible to lose the advantages to the competition? Are areas of the organization likely to bear significant cost increases?

Corporate identity symbols

Organizations go to great trouble to strengthen their corporate image by doing good deeds and filling needed community services.

A key *strength* question is: How can we make our company logo something employees can take pride in?

Key *vulnerability* questions would be: What circumstances could cause our symbols to lose their value? What will be the effect of growing ethnic pride be on symbols like "Redskins" or sleeping Mexicans, or the logos of Sambo's or Pillsbury?

Technology

Technology supports many, if not all, organizations in our society. In the computer wars of the last decade, terms like PC, laptop, and mainframe competed, each referring to somewhat different technologies. Mainframes served IBM and Digital Equipment Corp. (DEC) well for many years. However, while the capabilities and speed of PCs increased rapidly, mainframes became more specialized and lost their market share. The failure to recognize the importance of PCs made IBM and DEC vulnerable, and their CEOs — Akers and Olsen — subsequently lost their jobs.

Relevant *strength* questions include: Are our technologies state of the art? Can we apply them to other areas?

A relevant *vulnerability* question is: What developments might render current technologies obsolete?

Special abilities

Organizations gain the reputation of doing something exceptionally well because of their knowledgeable people, their way of doing business, or their structure. Some people have specialized skills and qualities crucial to the organization's reputation; they are either not easily replaced or are irreplaceable. Geologists have abilities crucial to oil exploration. Programmers have abilities crucial to the software industry.

Relevant *strength* questions include: Are these abilities available in ample quantity at a reasonable rate? Are we able to preserve and enhance our special-ability requirements through in-service training?

Relevant *vulnerability* questions would be: Are schools turning out people with the needed abilities? Might our specialists defect? Why?

A good example of the kinds of analyses that may be derived from employing the issues vulnerability audit is given in Appendix D. The example comes from an exercise conducted by the authors at the leadership training conference for senior managers of a multi-national petroleum corporation.

Summary

An issues vulnerability audit improves the judgment of organizational leaders. It forces them to think "outside the box," viewing their organization as others might view it. Also, the audit makes them aware of their dependence on external forces, which in turn helps them to anticipate change and spot emerging issues. By identifying threats, leaders have time to monitor situations, review options, and prepare issue briefs. Including managers from different areas improves interdepartmental communication.

The issues vulnerability audit process improves the efficiency of the strategic trend intelligence system. Some organizations try to monitor everything in the environment, wasting both time and resources. Others do not monitor the right areas, thereby exposing the organization to unnecessary risks. The issues vulnerability audit concentrates on the most important environmental areas for the organization: the ones that may cause the biggest headaches.

The importance of critical issues is further communicated through the preparation of an Issue Brief. The methodology is explained in the next chapter.

CHAPTER SEVEN

Power Tool Number Five

Issue Briefs

Establishing a strategic trend intelligence system and conducting an issues vulnerability audit provide raw data. Raw data is a far cry from strategic information to bring to management. Recall from Chapter 1 that strategic thinking results, in part, from translating data into information, information into conclusions, and conclusions into action.

An issue brief is a clear, concise introductory paper about an emerging issue. Issue briefs should be no longer than two, single-spaced pages, in a standard format. An issue brief is not a white paper. It is not intended to cover everything, only to introduce members of a steering committee to an emerging issue. It provides only enough information for a committee member to make an informed judgment on the issue's significance to the organization.

Anatomy of an Issue Brief

The components of a model issue brief are a summary statement of the issue, a description of its background, a listing of the forces driving it, a projection of its future, and a projection of its implications for the organization. Airline industry examples for each component are outlined below, while a fully assembled issue brief is presented in Appendix E.

Issue focus

The introductory statement should capture the essence of the issue in two-to-three lines. It should be provocative, challenging corporate policy.

Consider some examples:

Issue: Stress in the workplace

Issue focus: A consensus is developing that employee stress is costly, and workplace conditions are a contributing factor. Should the organization review conditions to identify and alleviate stress?

Issue: Contracting out

Issue focus: Both workers and management desire more certain employer-employee relationships. Competitive pressures, the need to downsize, restrictive career designs, and productivity demands cause both sides to consider the use of outside contractors. Can the organization afford to rely on its staffing strategies in the mid- and long-term?

Issue: Information technology (IT)

Issue focus: Information technology is increasingly recognized as central to organizational strategy. Does the organization's vision take full advantage of the wide-ranging business potential offered by existing and emerging computer resources?

Background

The background should provide an overview of the issue's recent development. Typically, a background section will include specific events behind the issue and the ways other organizations are dealing (or not dealing) with the issue. It should bring the reader up to date without overburdening the reader with detail.

Issue: Teleconferencing

Background: In the 23 years that AT&T has been in the teleconferencing business, growth has been slight because of the lack of competition, and the high cost of purchasing, leasing, and operating equipment. AT&T has historically monopolized the industry and given low priority to marketing its teleconferencing services. Business people place a high premium on face-to-face meetings and have traditionally favored air travel as more cost effective.

Issue: Bankruptcy reform

Background: In 1978, Congress enacted a sweeping reform of bankruptcy law that, among other things, deleted the insolvency test and gave judges the power to decide contract and damage suits. As a consequence, bankruptcy filings increased nearly threefold from January 1979 to July 1984.

Issue: Teletext and video text

Background: The revolution in microelectronics has produced two new technologies with important implications for marketing and distribution. Teletext and video text disseminate verbal and pictorial information to consumers who use them selectively. Teletext is a one-way service broadcast as part of the television signal.

Subscribers use a keypad — often part of their remote control unit — to select which information to display. Video text is a two-way service: users are able to send, as well as receive information.

Driving forces

In the section on driving forces, the background information should be linked to trends and events that are influencing the issue. This section includes initiatives by special-interest groups, lobbyists, and legislatures, as well as behaviors of other primary and secondary stakeholders. It should be kept to one paragraph, as free of jargon as possible.

Issue: Teleconferencing

Driving forces: Significant changes have begun toward lowering purchasing, leasing, and operating costs. A high-quality video teleconferencing system can be purchased for about $250,000. Transmission costs for some teleconferencing technologies have fallen as much as ten-fold: from $1,000 to $100 per hour, while quality and variety have improved.

"Real-time" computer networking is growing in popularity as both audio and visual aspects have been become more user friendly. Aggressive marketing of picture phones has begun. Outlets offering international teleconferencing services are expanding. Decision makers are reevaluating the benefits of face-to-face meetings because of rising travel costs, increased sensitivity about work time, and a growing emphasis on international trade.

Issue: Re-regulation

Driving forces: Subtle re-regulation initiatives result from a weakening of the political will to push deregulation further, and a strengthening of the political opposition. The lack of free-market support in the recent debates over the telecommunications and natural gas industries are ready evidence. Airlines are weary from the industry's worst-ever decline. Re-regulation could return air travel to its past as high-cost transport for the privileged, with an even greater shake-out than has already occurred.

Issue: The Tylenol syndrome

Driving forces: The public's confidence in the business community to act in a responsible manner is declining significantly as copycat tampering grows in variety and frequency. McDonald's beef has been spiked; bottles of Visine have been found to contain hydrochloric acid despite their tamper-proof seals being intact at time of purchase. The most recent claims in June 1993 that Diet Pepsi cans contained syringes indicate that the problem continues.

Future prospects

In this section, trends are extrapolated and sound forecasts are included. Even if the future of an issue remains unclear, an attempt should be made to describe possible scenarios.

Issue: Air quality in the workplace

Future prospects: Local smoking ordinances will proliferate. Airplanes may come to be seen as comparable to other workplace environments, with standards set to protect the crew. Coincidental to the discussion of more exotic pollutants like radon, debate over cabin air quality will increasingly involve humidity and air contaminants.

Issue: Teleconferencing

Future prospects: The future of teleconferencing, and, in particular, the degree to which it will disrupt demand for travel, is uncertain. Potential growth is considerable. Experts agree that teleconferencing will see its greatest growth in the second half of the decade, resulting from confusion over airline fares and lobbying by consumer advocates and other special interest groups. Estimates are that teleconferencing may eventually displace 20 - 25 percent of corporate travel budgets.

Issue: The Tylenol syndrome

Future prospects: If tampering increases in frequency or severity, regulations could follow. If business increases its diligent surveillance, regulation could be avoided.

Implications

So far, the issue brief has helped the manager discover what the issue is, where it came from, what is driving it, and has provided some thoughts on how it will develop. The last section of the brief asks why the issue is important to the organization.

Although all of the potential implications may not be readily discernible, it is important that some connection be made between where the issue appears headed and the business of the organization.

Issue: The Tylenol Syndrome

Implications: The security of the food and beverages provided in flight is at issue. Airlines may find it necessary to develop sets of prophylactic measures to deal with actual or suspected cases of tampering and with blackmail attempts.

Issue: Air quality in the workplace

Implications: The mid-term future will likely yield a steady increase in smoking ordinances. Airplanes may come to be seen as other workplace environments and standards may be set without input from airline management. New rules on cabin air quality could require the airline to renovate the ventilation system and install costly monitoring equipment aboard each aircraft.

Issue: Teleconferencing

Implications: If teleconferencing costs fall and the quality of the technology improves as forecasted, airlines may find their larger corporate clients restricting air travel in favor of teleconferencing. Smaller firms may follow suit as other practical systems become available.

Summary

So far we have discussed how to scan and monitor trends, reveal issues through an issues vulnerability audit, and use the resulting information to write an issue brief.

The wise issue manager will remember the story of the baseball player at bat in the bottom of the ninth, score tied, bases loaded with a 3-and-2 count. As he lets the ball whiz by, he turns anxiously to the umpire and passionately implores, "What was it?" The umpire replies, "It ain't nothing till I call it." No matter how strongly the issues manager regards an issue, it comes to nothing until given a priority by the senior management steering committee. Another tool to help assess the priority of an issue, the Delphi Rating Method, is described in the next chapter.

CHAPTER EIGHT

Power Tool Number Six

Delphi Rating Method

Anticipatory issue management requires adherence to the KISS principle (Keep It Simple, Stupid). The goal is to obtain the best thinking your steering committee members are capable of, in the least amount of time. The organization's efforts and resources should be directed toward issues that the committee agrees are worthy of a serious financial and moral judgment.

Once the CEO has endorsed a program, the issue manager must avoid initial exuberance by other managers who try to demonstrate their commitment with wild issue hunting. (Remember, if you provide a child with a hammer, everything looks like a nail.) Every unresolved management concern, from secretarial empowerment to the latest fad, will beg to be treated as an issue. The issue manager will continually need to reiterate the definition of an issue:

An issue is an internal or external development that could affect the organization's performance. The issue is one to which the organization must respond in an orderly fashion and over which it may reasonably expect to exert influence.

Which Category?

Sorting issues by their effect on the organization and the organization's ability to influence the issue is one of the most important components of issue management. Prioritization deals with four key questions:

- Will the issue escalate?
- Will it affect the organization?
- Can the organization influence the issue?
- Should it do so?

Prioritization identifies three types of issues: those requiring action (Category I), those that for reasons of maturity or inability to manage are not worthy of action planning at present (Category II), and those requiring no action (Category III). Category I issues will be discussed within the framework of the 10-step IM model described in the next chapter. Category II issues cannot effectively be managed but may still require policy statements. Category III issues need to be monitored and periodically revisited.

Applying a Tool of the Futurists — The Delphi

When dealing with an emerging issue, the steering committee is likely to find wide disparity among managers' knowledge of the issue. Differing perspectives of where the issue is headed and what its impact on the organization will be, may engender a wide range of responses. Some managers are louder, stronger, and more forceful than others — which could upset priorities.

The use of a simplified, one-round version of the Delphi technique overcomes some of these concerns. When managers evaluate issues independently, as with the Delphi technique, they are assured that each of their perspectives will be fairly represented.

Approximately three weeks before the group meets, the issue manager should provide committee members with the issue briefs (see Appendix E) and delphi issue rating forms (see Appendix F). Following directions on the rating form, members will use a "can-should" formula to place issues along a continuum. On the positive side, the spectrum starts with a position that the organization, if it acts now, will have the widest array of options. On the opposite side of the continuum is the position that the organization would be negligent not to act now. Treating an issue at this end is a judgment that elevates the issue to Category I. Divergent perspectives are important to capture in discussion.

A week before the meeting, each member should return the rating forms to the issue manager for tabulation, so the manager can quickly see the extent of agreement among the members.

At the meeting, the facilitator (the issue manager or the officer to whom the manager reports) should draw out the widest points of disagreement and ask the opponents to discuss their views. Since no one is yet responsible for the issue, the discussion can be open and objective. Working through areas of wide divergence is an effective means of bringing the other managers into the discussion and fleshing out the issue.

The Delphi Rating Sheet

The rating document should be kept as simple as possible. The rating form shown as Appendix F has been used with much success.

The **issue focus** restates the introductory statement found in the issue brief.

The **stage of development** section asks respondents to place the issue on the issue life cycle. Disagreement among managers and the ensuing discussion will help prioritize the issues.

The **issue evaluation** asks respondents to evaluate the degree to which the organization can and should influence the issue, if it were to start immediately. As can be seen in the consensus form that follows, the difference between can and should provides for a broad range of response.

Opinions from the issue evaluation are graphically shown in the **priority assignment** section.

The **degree of familiarity** section asks respondents to place their understanding of the issue along a continuum. The more familiar respondents are with an emerging issue, the more they can contribute.

The **additional observation** section gives respondents an opportunity to share further comments. The comments might include special insights, other activity within the organization, and initiatives by other organizations.

Once the ratings forms have been completed and returned, a picture forms of the degree of convergence among the managers. A consensus report is produced that contains all the ratings, with each contributor being identified by initials. A sample Delphi Rating Sheet and Consensus Report are presented in Appendix F.

At the meeting, the facilitator needs only to display a chart of the consensus results before opening the issue for discussion. The most divergent voters should be encouraged to discuss their rationale, which will allow the facilitator to draw the rest of the group into a lively exchange. Members of the issue management group should be present and prepared to offer additional information from the strategic trend intelligence system.

Choosing an Owner

Once the steering committee decides that the organization can and should influence an issue (Category I), an issue owner is designated. Usually a senior officer closely aligned with the issue, the issue owner takes responsibility for the action team and is responsible for the team's report to the steering committee and the CEO. Many times the issue owner nominates a representative to assist in managing the team.

For Category II issues, the concern is not management and influence outside the organization, but rather containment and compliance within. The organization may not be able to influence the issue externally, given the present circumstances, but it is of sufficient importance to require an internal structural or policy readjustment. The Americans with Disabilities Act could not be managed externally in 1992. Internal policies on hiring and architectural adjustments were necessary and needed to be communicated to the whole organization.

Category III issues require no action at present. However, they are of sufficient importance to continue monitoring. It is important to remember that shifts may occur externally (e.g., legislative or regulatory changes) or internally (e.g., new marketing schemes, products, or acquisitions). If such shifts appear, Category III issues should be reevaluated, and a new issue brief should be drafted and submitted to the steering committee. The iterative nature of the process assures that issues are not lost.

Summary

We have examined anticipatory issue management through environmental scanning and monitoring, the issue life cycle, issue vulnerability audits, issue briefs, and the initial involvement of the steering committee in prioritizing issues. In the next chapter, the reader will learn how to apply the 10-Step Issue Management Process to assure that Category I issues are handled in a systematic manner.

CHAPTER NINE

Power Tool Number Seven

The 10-Step Issue Management Process

Issue management allows one to anticipate and manage issues that could drastically affect organizational performance. A systematic issue management program provides valuable lead time to evaluate options thoroughly, allocate resources effectively, and position the organization creatively so that it may act in an orderly and prudent manner.

The IM process includes activities to give an organization state-of-the-art readiness through cross-disciplinary work teams, in-depth issue analysis, and solid action plans. A discussion of the steps follows. The reader also will find case studies in issue management in Appendix G.

Step 1. Designate an Issue Owner

The cross-disciplinary nature of issue analysis requires well-defined roles and a realistic timetable to identify issues, determine their significance, and evaluate responses available under different scenarios. Ownership of an issue should reside with the senior officer most closely aligned with it. Responsibility for follow-up and facilitation remains with the chair of the issue management committee.

Step 2. Form an Action Team

Many issues management programs fail because they do not involve the right people. The need for issues management grew from a realization of the complexity of the external environment, where issues do not fit into predetermined boxes. Boxes work no better in the internal world of the organization.

Issues will necessarily affect many areas of the organization to differing degrees. A determination must be made of who in the organization has the most stake in the issue and what departments should take part in the goal planning and implementation. Teams may vary from three people to as many as 30, depending on the issue's importance.

No one waits to be put on an action team. The invitation should come from the prospective team member's boss. It should describe the IM process, its importance to the company, and what will be expected from involvement.

Action team members are front-line people. It is important that they be asked to contribute ideas early in the process.

Consider an airline's action team discussing cabin safety. Initially, the discussion centers on crew communications, smoke detectors, floor lighting, limitations on carry-on luggage, flammability of seat fabric and wall liners, and placement of handicapped people in aisle seats near the exit. Petroleum engineers from the maintenance facility mention attempts by the U.S. Department of Transportation and the Federal Aviation Administration (FAA) to introduce Avgard, a chemical additive, into jet fuel. No one else in the group has heard of Avgard. Further discussion reveals the significant implications of Avgard on cabin safety.

Keep all team meetings short, no longer than an hour. Establish an agenda and tell participants in advance what will be expected of them individually.

Step 3. Conduct a Situational Assessment

At the first meeting, explain why each member was selected, why the company needs to be ahead of the issue, and why cooperation is important. Ask each person to complete the issue analysis worksheet discussed in Chapter 11.

Define the Issue

One of the first tasks of the team will be to define the issue from the company's perspective. When an issue is confronted early in its life cycle, not only can the company resolve the issue, but also it can resolve the issue to the company's advantage and the best interests of society. The issue might be the need to provide quality customer service. The company's concern might be how to provide such service without requiring more employees.

Often an issue's significance depends on how it is viewed by those outside the organization. Early in the life cycle, it is easy to dismiss an issue as insignificant. Denial only delays matters and may put the organization in jeopardy. Nearly all major issues have long gestation periods. Public policy issues may take decades to develop. The Consumer Product Safety Commission took years to become viable. Equal opportunity in the workforce took more than 30 years to become law.

Dealing with an issue early in its life cycle allows the company to define it. Waiting until an issue (fair credit, equal opportunity, universal healthcare access) is defined by stakeholders results in an issue definition that may be problematic. The company may then be seen as a villain when it does take a position on such an issue. The tardy manner in which business has entered the debate on a great many issues (e.g., breast implants, auto safety), has contributed to the perception that business people are hiding something.

Gathering information

The next step after defining an issue is determining its background to a much deeper level than in the issue brief. What developments have led to the issue's present position in the life cycle? What is its likely future direction? Answers might be found in the organization's environmental scanning database, but most often further searching is required — possibly using such databases as Dialogue, BRS, ABI Inform, Nexis, and Lexis.

Ask team members for their perspectives. In the case of the airplane cabin safety issue, the discussion centered on communications, lighting, smoke detectors and flame retardants, until team members from the maintenance center revealed that Avgard constituted the real threat. Their contribution led the team to participate in a successful effort to eliminate use of the additive.

Step 4. Study the Results

If a company is successful in influencing an issue — as with airplane cabin safety — the issue will go unnoticed outside the industry. When an issue is resolved successfully, very little is written about it, even inside the industry.

The resolution of an issue — the defeat of a bill or the avoidance of company restrictions or penalties — should not imply business as usual. Issues that have drawn attention from a variety of interests do not just go away, but tend to reappear in modified form. It is in the company's interest to continue to assess, and possibly even modify, its behavior in the way the issue would have required. Meanwhile, the issue management team continues to monitor the issue.

Following the passage of major legislation, a program must be developed to assure compliance and avoid costly penalties. The legal department will need to interpret the legislation to specify the organization's exact responsibilities. Departments affected by the legislation should oversee the program, making sure that it is implemented throughout the company (e.g., human resources handles Equal Employment Opportunity Commission compliance; customer service handles consumer issues; operations handles pollution control). Public relations and public affairs still have their work to do, but now they have a base from which to work.

For the majority of organizations that have an overall strategic plan, it is vital to consider the impact of each resolved issue on that plan. Failure to do so may render the plan useless, as staff time is absorbed into accommodating the issue.

Step 5. Identify Stakeholders

Understanding the stakeholders is crucial to managing an issue, which further depends on how quickly and how effectively the organization handles stakeholder concerns. If an organization waits to act until an issue matures (reaches the media) the issue has been interpreted by someone else and may defy management. Success requires influencing stakeholders to change their perceptions while those perceptions can still be changed.

Primary and secondary stakeholders

Clarkson (1993) defines stakeholders as individuals or groups who claim ownership rights or other interests in an organization and its past, present, or future activities. Stakeholders with similar interests are classified as belonging to the same group (e.g., employees, customers, and shareholders).

Clarkson divides stakeholders into primary and secondary groups. Primary stakeholders are those an organization needs for survival. They are typically shareholders, employees, customers, vendors, suppliers, distributors, and governments.

Secondary stakeholders, which include special interest groups and the media, are not directly involved in the activities of an organization. Their importance generally lies in their ability to mobilize public opinion.

Stakeholder influence

Stakeholders can influence an organization in subtle and serious ways. Customers can stop buying, suppliers can refuse to supply, shareholders can organize their vote, and unions can second-guess management decisions.

The organization must create and maintain value for its primary stakeholders. Failure to do so could result in failure of the organization. When investors did not provide sufficient capital to particular savings and loans institutions, the institutions failed. Failure of Dow Corning to satisfy its customers and the media meant withdrawing from a lucrative breast-implant business. A.H. Robins and Manville Corporation found themselves bankrupt because they failed to acknowledge their customers' health concerns. Firestone Tire & Rubber continued to manufacture and sell its Radial 500 tire in spite of convincing evidence that the tire was defective and dangerous. The result was a $135 million liability.

Secondary stakeholders can mold primary stakeholder opinion. Special interest groups with substantial war chests can raise an issue from relative obscurity to high visibility quickly. Community organizer Saul Alinsky had nonprofit organizations give him their voting proxies in situations where he felt that corporations were not being socially responsible. He gained access to shareholder meetings and the media (Alinsky, 1971). Black community leaders in Rochester, NY, adopted this technique to force Eastman Kodak Corp. to alter its promotion and hiring practices (Heath and Nelson, 1986).

Redefining issues

Background issues can be elevated to the level of primary issues — like dividends, stock prices, and product quality — by the actions of secondary stakeholders. Nestlé Corporation's marketing of baby formula in Third World countries was attacked by the World Health Organization (WHO), the Infant Formula Action Coalition (INFACT), and the Interfaith Center for Corporate Responsibility (ICCR) over unsavory marketing techniques and failure to address sanitation problems in the countries where it was marketed. The issue was raised to such visibility that primary stakeholders responded with alarm. Customers throughout the U.S. and Europe boycotted Nestlé's products. Regulators placed voluntary restrictions on advertising and marketing techniques.

This transition of an issue from society to the organizational level is critical. An issue like equal opportunity begins as a social issue. When the 1963 Equal Pay Act was passed, corporations considered it primarily a social issue. For 13 years, Sears, Roebuck and Co. continued to pay women a 1 percent commission on sales of fine furs costing many thousands of dollars while paying men a 9 percent commission on sales of plumbing equipment of similar value. In the end, the government required Sears to provide female sales staff members with a $50 million pay adjustment.

To many managers, social issues have little to do with how they run their business. Managers are trained in production, marketing, finance, accounting, advertising, operations, and human resources. They understand issues in the context of these tasks and in many instances do not consider the broader social consequences of their decisions.

Forgotten stakeholders

Organizations are expected by society to fulfill a variety of obligations, which include making sure that all stakeholders are heard. The absence of important stakeholders in considering issues can be disastrous. In the case of high-voltage power lines, the absence of the academic and scientific community from early discussions led to gross misrepresentation by the media, influencing rate payers to protest the location of power lines near their homes.

Effective stakeholder analysis begins in the emerging-issue phase with the questions:

- Who are the primary and secondary stakeholders of this issue?
- What is their involvement?
- What are their positions?
- How do their positions differ? Why?
- How are they likely to affect the issue?
- Are there important stakeholders not yet involved in the issue?

Answers may be found by:

- Conducting stakeholder focus groups for customers, employees, and vendors
- Reviewing publications of special interest groups
- Conducting surveys

Rating stakeholders is a good way to improve information gathering. Sort stakeholders into the following categories:

- Those critical to dealing effectively with the issue and are already involved
- Those critical to dealing effectively with the issue but not yet involved
- Those important to dealing with the issue and are already involved
- Those important to dealing with the issue but not yet involved
- Those involved but not important to dealing with the issue
- Those not involved and not important to dealing with the issue

Although simplistic, this method assures accounting of each stakeholder.

Step 6. Formalize a Company Position

Developing a position should flow directly from issue analysis, and discussions with stakeholders and internal sources. The position statement drafted by the action team should:

- Be clear and concise
- State where the company stands on the issue
- Direct the company toward the desired outcome
- Take obstacles into consideration

Step 7. Develop Stakeholders' Objectives

Since the agenda of each stakeholder will vary, each will need individualized help in developing a set of objectives that support the organization's position. With legislators and bureaucrats, the objective might be to assist them with timely, accurate, and balanced information. With public interest groups, it might be establishing liaisons, becoming a trusted source of information.

Step 8. Develop Organizational Objectives

Resolving an issue often requires that the company change the way it makes, delivers, or markets products and services. Once alternative action plans have been decided on, they must be tested against a clear set of criteria that include their impact on each stakeholder group.

Strengths: What advantages are there?

Vulnerability: What are the risks? What contingencies are available?

Validity: Are the underlying assumptions realistic?

Feasibility: Does the organization have the needed skills, resources, and commitment?

Ease: Can the organization implement the strategy easily?

Consistency: Is the action plan externally and internally consistent?

Timing: When should we act? When will we see the benefits?

Can the organization obtain those resources it does not have already? Can its structure accommodate the plan? What new structures may be needed?

Action plans are, by design, broad courses of action to be pursued over an extended period of time. Details are left for the implementation phase.

Sara Lee's solution

If its employees are experiencing discomfort in the work environment (e.g., repetitive stress injuries or carpal tunnel syndrome from using computer keyboards or decorating cakes), a company must go beyond standard public relations solutions to set clear objectives for relieving the problem. Sara Lee's response to repetitive stress complaints at its cake-decorating operation is a classic example. Rather than dismissing employee complaints as attempts to avoid work or take time off, Sara Lee hired a physician to observe the workers and make recommendations. Sara Lee also hired an ergonomics engineer to evaluate the assembly line. Recommendations from the doctor and the engineer were put into action. Complaints of repetitive stress decreased 80 percent.

Step 9. Implement the Action Plan

A successful organizational objectives session produces a specific set of ideas to implement over a specific period of time. It identifies specific resources needed to implement each of them. Attention should be concentrated on:

- Structural changes that need to be made and goals to carry out
- Individual and departmental responsibilities
- Timetables
- Evaluation methods
- Incentives for success

Implementation is the doing process. While people tend to expect implementation to unfold without any misdirection, the real world does not work that way. Introducing change means overcoming resistance to change.

Articulating the company position to stakeholders requires an action plan of several parts:

Establish a communications program

Without a communications program based on thorough research, professional communication skills, and skillful use of resources, the action plan will be stillborn. The best strategies are useless without good tactics.

Cooperate with other companies

Other companies within the industry or in other industries may have similar vulnerabilities but not have entered the debate. Informing them of the situation and involving them in a coalition can contribute greatly to resolving the issue.

Use quantitative data

Attempts to influence issues simply by contributing to someone's political action committee (PAC) are yielding fewer results. The importance of meaningful quantitative data cannot be overstated. Having taken the time to consider the issue, now is the time for the organization to put the knowledge it has gained into a white paper.

Involve company officers

Traditionally, organizations have felt well represented if they sent their public relations officer to do the talking. Important issues, particularly technical ones, deserve the involvement of other officers. Sending a line manager to discuss an issue with a politician or leader of a special interest group has far greater impact than sending someone from public relations.

Build credibility

Credibility is easily lost and seldom regained. With all stakeholders be prepared, listen, be reasonable, and make appropriate concessions.

Step 10. Monitor and Fine-tune

Stakeholder and organizational objectives should be quantifiable, if possible, so that assessment can begin immediately once the action plan is initiated.

Focus groups and interviews may suffice to determine if stakeholders have moved in the desired direction. If not, the action team should reconvene. It may be advisable anyway to reconvene the team on a monthly or bi-monthly basis to monitor progress on the issue, review new data, and consider fine-tuning.

The Final Litmus Test

Does the company have the ability to act effectively? Does it have the commitment? Action team members or other managers may have responsibilities that run counter to the proposed actions.

Are the actions appropriate? Answering this guards against undertaking an action plan that conflicts with the organization's primary role of providing goods and services.

Are the actions in society's best interests? What seems good for the organization may have hidden costs. Acting early in the issue life cycle requires that the organization understand what is good for society. While an action plan may be desirable from a profit-and-loss standpoint, the true test is to look at the plan from the outside-in. How are the major stakeholders likely to view the results?

Although coalition building is often a cost-effective way to deal with an issue, care should be taken on who to involve. United Airlines' analysis of the VDT issue initially suggested including manufacturers like IBM and Digital Equipment Corp. (DEC). A closer look showed that users (airlines, banks, insurance companies) had a much different stake than manufacturers, who could indeed benefit from regulations.

Summary

As with any business project, the bottom line is cost. Issue management is not cheap. Attempting to manage an issue is, at best, a gamble. Without convincing evidence that the benefits exceed the costs, managers will fail to commit themselves fully and the organization may be forced to abandon the project. One must always weigh how much a given plan will benefit society, reduce liabilities, and further corporate objectives.

CHAPTER TEN

Power Tool Number 8

The Issue Accountability Model

Understanding the movement of information through an organization goes beyond delineating the phases of the issues management process. To make issues management part of the organizational mind-set, one must make it part of the management structure.

The Issue Accountability Model shows the movement of strategic information from outside the organization to various decision gates within the organization. Without such a road map, many companies find themselves befuddled by an issue for which ample information already exists somewhere in the organization. Also, many in-house programs fail because the information languishes in a division or departmental file with no system to monitor its status or to bring it to the attention of the necessary people.

Understanding the flow of information through an organization is central to the successful implementation of an in-house issues management program. The structure should be kept simple. Management's time is at a premium. Although the IM process has significant bottom-line potential, it need not be complicated, cumbersome, or intrusive on day-to-day operations. Figure 10.1 shows the flow of information and the responsibilities that apply at each point.

1. The anticipatory management function

The anticipatory manager's responsibilities include the following activities:

- Maintain the strategic trend intelligence system
- Identify issues from numerous sources
- Analyze trend information to develop issue briefs to be considered by the steering committee

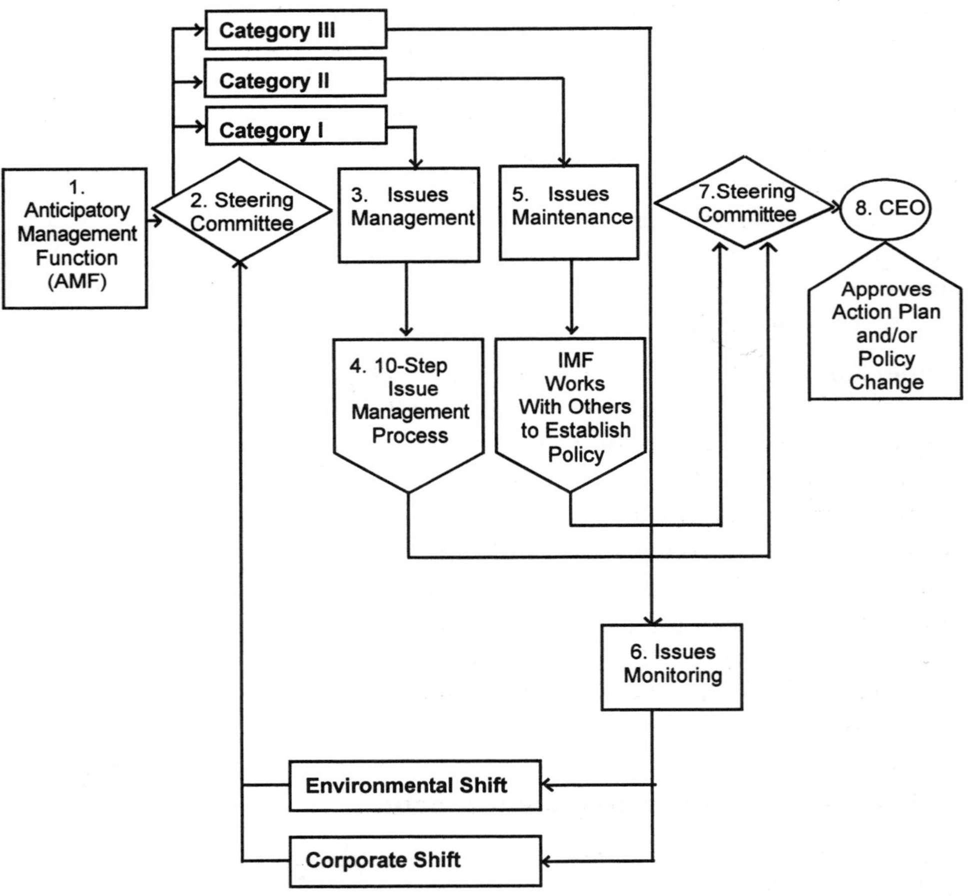

Figure 10.1 The Issue Accountability Model.

2. Steering committee

The steering committee is selected by the CEO to screen and prioritize emerging issues presented by the issues management staff. Individuals selected for this committee generally report directly to the CEO. They possess not only an in-depth knowledge of the organization, but also a broad perspective on the external forces which influence it. They must:

- Review issue briefs prepared by the issues management staff
- Determine implications and degree of organizational opportunity or vulnerability
- Use specific criteria to rate issues on probability of occurrence, impact, and degree to which the organization can and should influence them
- Determine the degree of organizational involvement, based on consensus opinion (i.e., sort issues into categories I, II, or III)

3. Issues Management

If an issue has been rated a Category I, it will likely continue in the direction it is headed and its impact on the organization will be high. The organization should attempt to influence either its direction or its effects on the organization. Responsibility for resolving the issue must rest at the senior management level. To relegate responsibility to a lower level is to belie the rating scheme and the organizational commitment.

4. 10-step IM model

The organization analyzes the issue using the 10-step IM methodology that is discussed in Chapter 9.

Once the steering committee determines an issue to be Category I, it assigns issue ownership by determining the department that could most benefit from or be hurt by the issue. The officer responsible for that area is designated the "owner." Ownership does not imply that work on the issue should be carried out exclusively within the owner's department. Establishing ownership is merely the first step in preparing Category I issues for management. While a senior manager may own the issue and be responsible to the CEO for its successful resolution, the manager may appoint someone else as chair of the action team. The issues manager works with the chair to select the action team, set the agenda, and facilitate team meetings as necessary.

5. Issues Maintenance

Should the steering committee classify the issue as Category II, that is, an issue that does not require management by an action team — the committee begins the process of policy formulation. Other departments may need to be involved so that the internal position is consistent with the issue's status.

6. Issues monitoring

The monitoring activity for issues in Category III concentrates on environmental shifts (changes in the direction of events, trends, and driving forces) and corporate shifts (changes in organizational policies, products, services, marketing strategies, or operating procedures) that could turn them into Category I issues needing analysis and management. Monitoring systematically collects and analyzes information related to the issue: changes in public attitudes, fiscal policy, regulations, legislation, or academic theory.

Understanding corporate and environmental shifts is the essence of anticipation. A major obstacle to anticipatory management is the evaluation of managers on efficient performance under relatively short-term targets, criteria being based on strict administration of resources. Whenever a new opportunity or threat is revealed, recognition will be resisted by managers whose performance will be affected by any shift in ongoing activities. (If it ain't broke, don't fix it.) For that reason, issues monitoring is a responsibility of the issue management staff. If the issue manager determines that an issue needs to be reconsidered as a Category I, the manager resubmits the issue to the steering committee.

7. Steering committee

At this stage, the steering committee reviews the action plan, including details of what is to be done, why it is to be done, who is to do it, when it is to be done, how much it will cost, and from where the money will come. Because many action plans involve cross-disciplinary work teams, it is crucial that all parties agree to the final presentation. The steering committee then forwards the plan to the CEO.

8. The Chief Executive Officer

The CEO is responsible for reviewing the action plan. The CEO will usually ask the issue owner and action team to present the plan at a steering committee meeting. Because the issue may not have fully crystallized, stakeholder positions, along with technical and operating objectives, should be presented to ensure everyone's involvement and commitment to the principles.

Summary

Issues confronting organizations need to be sorted into three categories: those requiring immediate external action, those requiring internal adjustments, and those requiring only further monitoring. The process of sorting issues and processing those belonging to the first two categories is discussed through two diagrams: one emphasizing the structure of issues management and the other the process of decision making. Regardless of the perspective, the work centers around an issues management group that discovers issues, and a steering committee that reviews those issues and recommends a course of action.

CHAPTER ELEVEN

Power Tool Number Nine

Issue Analysis Worksheet

Although having input from line and staff managers is essential to thorough issues analysis and situational assessment, the reality is their pay and their success does not come from managing issues. In reality managing an issue without their input would be shortsighted and narrow. Organizational structures rarely provide for rapid input and interaction between strategies and line managers. Further, in order to translate their observations into usable information, managers need a conceptual framework that enables them to fit their experience into the overall process.

The information the worksheet seeks is requested in a simplified format. Once a manager has been invited to participate on an action team because of his or her proximity to the issue, it is necessary to accumulate information about the issue from them in a systematic way. Each manger on the action team is involved with an emerging issue in a slightly different fashion. Even externally oriented functions such as public relations and public affairs have different stakeholders that may be active on an issue. Completing the worksheet assures strategic information about the issue is obtained from each manager.

This worksheet is best used in developing organizational positions, programs, and action plans for dealing with current or emerging issues. The information obtained by completing the questions in this guide will inform the action team about what is known and unknown about the dynamics of the issue under investigation.

All questions are to be responded to from the perspective of department or function an action team member represents. A thorough understanding of an issue is critical to any strategy or action by the organization. What is the essence of the issue? Where did it come from? Who are the players? What is driving it? Where is it headed? What are the implications for the organization?

At the first meeting of the action team this worksheet is given to each team member and instructions for its use spelled out by the issue owner or an appointed representative. The worksheet is designed to be taken back to the member's department where help from others may prove useful. The worksheet is returned to the team captain after a reasonable period of time. The information from each worksheet is collected into a master document which then is made available to each member. All are encouraged to comment on the input from other members.

This conceptual framework is provided through the use of this worksheet which allows the managers to contribute valuable information about an emerging issue, even in cases when an issue is in its infancy.

Issue Analysis Worksheet

Issue being evaluated (insert issue focus from issue brief):

____

____

Issue owner(s): ________________________________

____

Action team member: ________________________________

Division/branch: ________________________________

Why is this issue of concern? ________________________________

____

Where is this issue on the management involvement life cycle?

Societal Expectations | Policy Agenda | Formalization | Social Control

?

TIME

Who are the main internal and external stakeholders on this issue?

Stakeholder: ________________________________

Position: ________________________________

Why are they important? ________________________________

Stakeholder: ________________________________

Position: ________________________________

Why are they important? ________________________________

Stakeholder: ________________________________

Position: ________________________________

Why are they important? ________________________________

Describe stakeholder behavior to date: ________________________________

____

____

Are there important stakeholders missing from the debate?

____

____

____

What are the potential impacts of this issue on the company's reputation?

Short term: ______________________________

____

Long term: ______________________________

____

Is this issue specific to the company? Does it have wider implications?

Company implications: ______________________________

____

External implications: ______________________________

____

Who are the key adversaries in this matter?

Name: ______________________________

Group: ______________________________

Name: ______________________________

Group: ______________________________

Describe their agendas or strategies:

____

____

____

____

Who are the allies on this issue? What are their agendas, strengths and strategies?

Names: ____________________

Group: ____________________

Strategies: ____________________

What is known about public opinion on this issue?

How firmly entrenched does it appear?

How is the public being informed about the issue?

Are there legal implications from the present status of the issue or the company's position?

How is the company perceived by stakeholders?
(on a 1-10 scale, 10 being very negatively)

1 · · · · · · · · · 10

Additional background information:

What have the employees been told about the issue?

____

____

____

What are the company's plans to inform employees?

____

____

____

What are the most significant dimensions of the issue? How might principal parties use them?

____

____

What appear to be the organization's strengths in this controversy?

____

____

What non-organizational resources are available for advice and counsel on the issue?

____

____

Are there actions that might diffuse or minimize the impact of the issue?

____

____

Are there opportunities for a coalition approach to the issue? Who might the allies be?

____

____

What actions, if any, ought to be taken to open dialogue?

Are there innovative initiatives available to the organization?

What special actions must be taken, by whom, to improve the organization's understanding of the issue?

What action steps are recommended to diffuse the issue?

What is the timetable for dealing effectively with the issue?

Vulnerability assessment

Using a scale from 1-10 (10 being the greatest vulnerability) indicate the company's vulnerability to:

——— Regulatory action	——— Community action
——— Lawsuits	——— Residential action
——— Employee morale	——— Commercial action
——— Legislation	——— Industrial action
——— Media criticism	——— Site action
——— Other:	——— Other:

Once the information has been compiled into a working issue manual, it can be assessed for next steps, additional information needs, and key assignments. The results of the issue analysis worksheet serve to input many parts of the 10- step IM process. It will be possible to make impact assessments over a broader spectrum of the organization, providing greater insight into the various stakeholder groups and their agendas. The analysis will contribute to stakeholder strategies and positions and organizational strategies and positions, and help in developing a comprehensive action plan for the organization.

CHAPTER TWELVE

Power Tool Number Ten

The Scenario Technique Applied to Anticipatory Management

The Scenario Technique

In Chapter 2, we explored strategic thinking that concentrates on synthesizing ideas, as contrasted with conventional problem solving. Traditional education emphasizes rote learning, memorization, and recall. The preferred method of exploration is trial and error; the thought patterns are rigid; the solutions linear.

In business, traditional education has meant an emphasis on maintaining the status quo and watching the competition. Managers pursue problem solving within a well-tried paradigm. They act rationally, given their view of the world. Change is only embraced when it draws heavily on accumulated wisdom. Hard decisions are made only where they do not challenge long-held assumptions. Using old solutions is like trying to repair an American car with metric tools. Sometimes the wrench will fit, but more often it will slip and the nuts will get stripped.

Managers need to embrace uncertainty and make it central to their reasoning. Uncertainty is not a temporary deviation from the predictable; it is a standard part of the modern business environment.

The Role of Scenarios

The purpose of scenarios is not to eliminate, but to illuminate uncertainty. No technique sets the stage for applying anticipatory techniques as well as scenarios. No technique approximates their results. Scenarios help determine ramifications of an issue's development along several alternative paths. They enable one to examine the implications of policy shifts.

Scenarios have been available to managers for many years, but their use in many organizations has not gone far enough. Too often, they are merely elaborate presentations of numbers for some point in the future: the price of oil in 2000; the rate of inflation over the next 10 years.

Scenarios are popular when managers do not have to make the final decision on which scenario to select. They are viewed by middle managers as games of no lasting consequence. To senior managers, whose jobs depend on guaranteeing stable growth and profitability, scenarios appear threatening: they have their jobs because they demonstrated good judgment under the existing paradigm. Their understanding of that paradigm is central to their self image.

The "Inner World" of Managers

By definition, anticipatory management — scanning and monitoring issues, and challenging assumptions — deals systematically with a world outside the organization. Tracking supply and demand, pricing, technology, competition, and regulation requires an outside-in perspective.

Outside-in thinking only becomes strategic thinking when it penetrates the "inner world" of managers, where the real decisions are made. Scenarios offer important additional information about the outer world. More significantly though, they can fundamentally alter perceptions, opening the mind to insights that were previously beyond reach. The breakthroughs come not from presenting impressive numbers or elaborate charts but from forcing managers to confront their assumptions about how their business works, challenging them to rebuild their obsolete models of the world.

An understanding of the typical managerial mind-set can transform scenarios from a threatening bogey into another use of anticipatory management. The human mind works by using its accumulated experience to construct an internal model of external reality. Decisions are based on alternatives found within the internal model, and alternatives to that model effectively do not exist. This phenomenon was discussed earlier through the metaphor of decision screens. Internal models develop a momentum over time: only information that supports the information gathered so far is accepted. Information that contradicts previous views, or simply does not fit the assumptions, is ignored. Rigid adherence to well-tried models leads to rapid obsolescence in a change-driven world.

Real-world issues are complex, dynamic creatures. Understanding and dealing with them requires tools — such as scenarios — that take into consideration the complex interactions of social, technological, economic, environmental, and political forces.

Scenarios	
are not...	**are more like...**
• Predictions of the future	• Descriptions of possible futures
• Variations on a chosen future	• Fundamentally different views of the future
• Vague	• Sharp, focused images

Figure 12.1 What scenarios are and are not.

Spyglass on the Future

Picture the future not as a straight line, but as a branching multitude of pathways, like the branches in an infinitely large tree. The tree is the "search space" of possible futures. Some parts of the tree represent likely events, others highly unlikely events. Scenarios pick out certain areas of the tree based on their likelihood of occurrence and the organization's strategic direction.

Care should be taken not to focus only on areas of apparent high likelihood, or the view of the future may collapse back to a straight line that does little more than extrapolate the past into the future. In a fractal universe, small events can have tremendous consequences ("the butterfly effect"). If scenarios are to truly assist managers in dealing with uncertainty, the unlikely must somehow be taken into account.

Wildcard scenarios are based on conditions that are unlikely to occur but would, if they did occur, have a tremendous effect on the organization. As we see in Figure 12.2, these scenarios lie outside the area of plausible futures. For example, 10 years ago, the dismantling of the USSR and the Eastern Bloc countries would have been wildcard scenarios. Planning for such developments can help managers deal with the improbable scenarios that do arise.

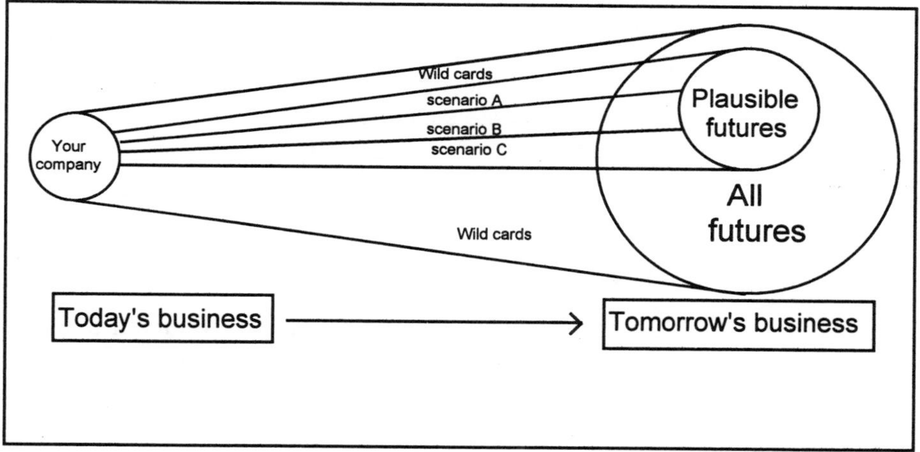

Figure 12.2. Spyglass on the future.

Creating Multiple Scenarios: One Approach

There are a number of ways to formulate multiple scenarios. We will illustrate several examples. The first approach frames a strategically important issue that needs to be thought through. We must specify the decision factors that need to be addressed, identify relevant external environmental forces, select scenario logics or stories about how the issue might unfold, create the logic or stories, and then think through the the implications of these scenarios for the organization. (See Figure 12.3)

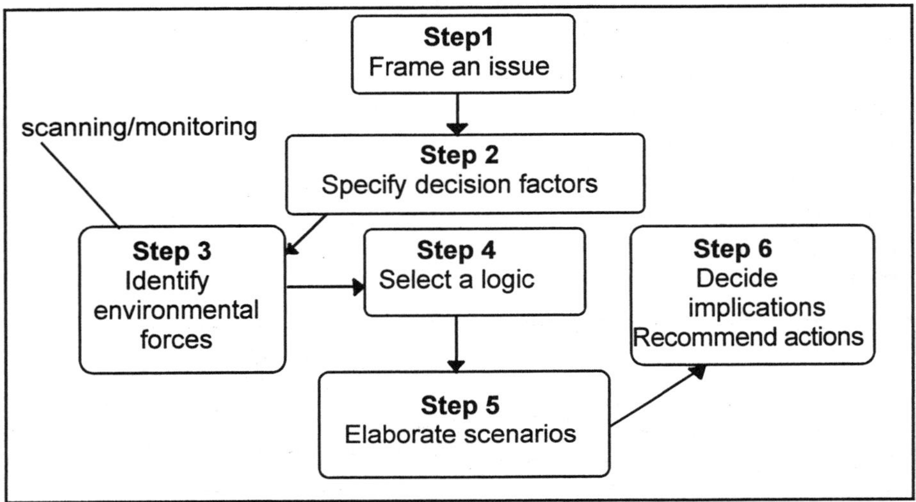

Figure 12.3. One approach to creating multiple scenarios.

1. Frame an issue

In this step, *we* must portray the issue in a way that highlights its significance to the organization. In the case of a large public utility in a region with poor air quality, the issue was described as follows:

> Given the poor air quality in our operating area, how is the utility contributing to the problem and what can the utility do to alleviate it?
>
> The air quality issue has several components with the common goals of mitigating adverse environmental or health effects. These components include:

- Air quality standards
- Visibility
- Acid rain
- Damage to lakes and rivers
- The greenhouse effect
- Toxic gases
- Fugitive dust from dry lake beds

2. Specify decision factors

Articulate the major decision factors that need to be addressed. In the case of the utility, these factors included the following questions:

- How can the level of contaminants emitted be reduced, by kind and by amount?
- How do the condition and age of burners and other equipment contribute to the problem?
- What are the present and emerging regulatory initiatives?
- Are cleaner power providers available?
- What costs are involved in replacement or retrofitting?
- How do the rate payers feel?
- How can public opinion be directed toward our best advantage?

Decision factors were broken down for each component of an issue, as determined in Step 1, (i.e., air quality standards, visibility, acid rain, etc.).

3. Identify local and global environmental forces

Identify and analyze the environmental forces driving each component of the issue in one direction or another. What forces might come into play, including social (attitudes toward pollution, lifestyles, stakeholder influence), technological (alternative fuels, fusion, ways to make existing equipment less polluting), economic (relative cost of energy sources, cost of adding new technologies, funding for equipment changes, impact on rate payers), environmental (condition of the ozone layer, airborne particulate matter), and political (mayoral and city council elections, internal politics)?

Consider air quality standards as a primary component of the overall air quality issue. Forces affecting the issue include:

- The increasing number of electric vehicles. California has passed a law that requires 10% of the vehicles sold in the state to be electric powered by 1997. Keeping these vehicles charged will require increasing output from the utility. Other states are considering similar legislation.
- A regulatory rule directs utilities to reduce nitrous oxide emissions by 75 percent in 10 years. This rule will require substantial equipment modifications.

4. Select a scenario logic or story line

The impact of environmental forces on the organization and the level of uncertainty help determine which scenario logics should be considered first. Selecting several will strengthen the resulting picture.

First, consider those forces that are most critical to the issue and possess the highest degree of uncertainty. Alternate logics will explain why and how these forces might take different paths to the future, helping one concentrate on where the decision points are and where the paths diverge.

Bear in mind that scenarios are not intended to be answers (what the pollution levels will be in 2005), but rather, they illuminate questions of how events might unfold, given the probable dynamics.

Give each scenario a descriptive and colorful title to convey the essence of what will happen. Book and movie titles can be useful sources. Titles can serve as reminders as the scenario plays itself out of what should be some of the concerns.

In our example, the utility selected two scenario logics based on technological considerations (retrofitting vs. repowering) and political considerations (being open to regulatory negotiation vs. being closed to negotiation).

Scenario A: "Penny wise and pound foolish"

Intractable regulators impose regulations requiring the utility to retrofit its power plants with scrubbers to reduce particulate emissions by a date in the near future. The utility and the regulatory board maintain their traditional antagonism.

Scenario B: What a difference a little time makes

The utility and the regulatory body work together to produce a mutually acceptable solution. Giving the utility a short reprieve on compliance will allow it to repower its plants, bringing entirely new technology on line to achieve an even more environmentally sound solution than retrofitting.

5. Elaborate scenarios

These scenarios need fleshing out into full-blown narratives that include dates (when events will occur, decisions will need to be made, options will disappear) and central players (who will be involved in the events, make the decisions, recognize the options while time remains).

6. Decide implications

The apparent implications of Scenario A are additional stress on existing facilities with no long-term benefits for the utility. The actions of both the utility and the regulatory board appear short-sighted and costly, as confrontation produces work for the lawyers but prevents anyone else from getting anything done. Meanwhile, retrofitting adds to the Greenhouse Effect. To the public, the regulatory board appears as the champion of clean air while the utility appears the foot-dragging bad boy.

Scenario B offers a sharply contrasting picture: Confrontation is avoided, and the utility saves millions of dollars in fuel costs. Meanwhile, ambient air quality improves and the Greenhouse Effect is minimized. Both the regulatory board and the utility appear as champions of clean air, and no one raises a fuss over the slightly longer implementation time.

A Second Example: Telecommunications

Another approach to developing scenarios is to focus on a strategic issue. List the forces that impact/define the issue. Rank these forces by the amount of impact they will have on the organization and the certainty of their occurring.

It is possible to generate scenarios for each combination of driving forces. The process can be quite involved and require much time to complete. However, for purposes of demonstration we will use two highly-ranked external forces.

Consider a global telecommunications company that must make important capital investment decisions. What will its market look like over the next 5-to-10 years?

1. List the driving forces

Begin by listing the driving forces that cause uncertainty in the industry (e.g., fuel costs, regulation, economic recession, political unrest, technological developments, or events like semi-conductor manufacturers forming a cartel).

2. Rank impact and uncertainty

Rank the driving forces by potential impact on the organization and degree of uncertainty of selecting the two forces that have the highest score on both counts: fuel costs and regulations.

Impact	Uncertainty
1. Local regulations	1. Fuel costs
2. Fuel costs	2. Local regulations
3. Depression	3. World peace
4. Semi-conductor cartel	4. Regional wars
5. Regional wars	5. Depression
6. World peace	6. Semi-conductor cartel

Figure 12.4 Ratings by a steering committee.

When fuel costs are high, organizations are more likely to use telecommunications because of the costs of air travel (all other things being equal). When fuel costs are low, airfares are low as well, and more people fly. If regulations are not standardized from one region to the next, equipment costs will rise because the company will be forced to conform to each local idiosyncrasy. If regulations are kept minimal, then a *de facto* global standard can be introduced, and equipment prices will fall.

3. Create multiple scenarios

As seen in Figure 12.5, four alternative scenarios can be created using the poles of the two selected driving forces (i.e., low or high local regulations, low or high fuel costs). In the "home alone" scenario, both travel and telecommunications are prohibitively expensive. In "video heaven," fewer people fly and more take advantage of low-cost, globally standardized telecommunications equipment. In "video

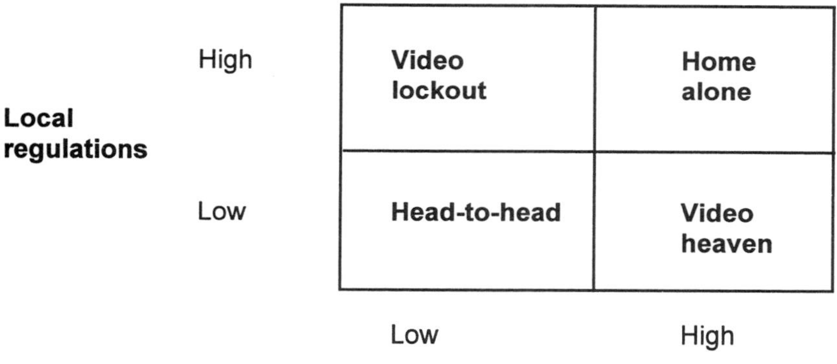

Figure 12.5. Alternative scenarios for a global telecommunications company.

lockout," cheap air fares make telecommunications relatively unattractive. In "head-to-head," the airline and telecommunications industries battle it out in fierce competition.

4. Create narratives

Now flesh the scenarios out so that each tells a story. Begin by identifying those events that would bring about each scenario and assign them tentative dates. Take the case of the "home alone" scenario: closed borders, increased regionalism, governmental action to lower fossil

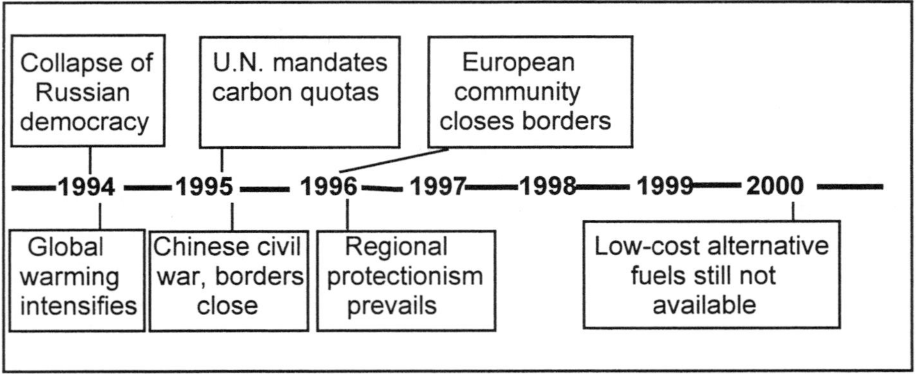

Figure 12.6. "Home-alone" time line.

fuel use, and failure to find cheap alternative fuels combine to raise fuel costs dramatically.

5. Determine implications

Determine the implications of each scenario and propose actions, debating the soundness of each action regardless of the scenario in which it originated. Or, select the most plausible scenario and plan for it, using the other scenarios for contingency planning.

The implications of the "home alone" scenario are that international companies will need to decentralize and avoid investing in expensive, high-tech equipment that cannot be standardized from region to region. The telecommunications company should try to ally with strong regional businesses and invest in low-tech equipment (i.e., broadcast towers, land lines, and fiber optics, rather than satellites).

The Product: Multiple Scenario Analysis

The authors led a scenario exercise with petroleum executives from a multinational company that yielded five scenarios. The scenarios explored the panorama of how regulation and fuel costs might play out in the international oil business. The resulting scenarios (Figure 12.7) are titled Big Squeeze, Shakeout, Boomtown, and Watch-out. A Wild Card scenario also was developed. Their implications and recommendations for action are described on the next page.

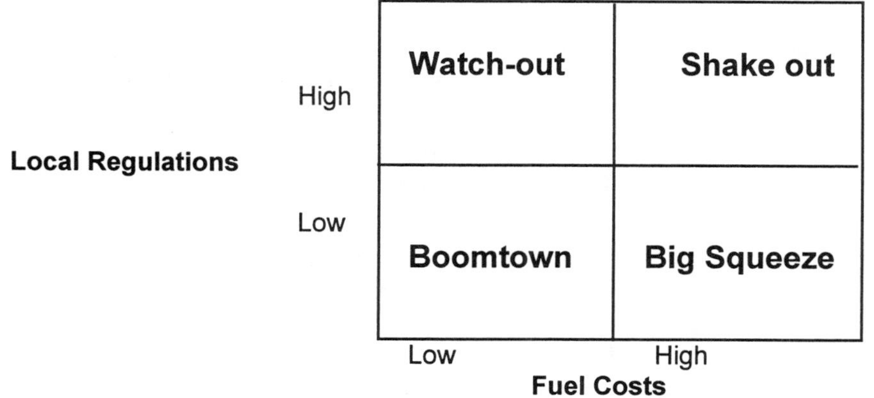

Figure 12.7 Scenarios for a multinational petroleum corporation.

Scenario 1: Squeeze (High fuel cost; low regulation)

1994 Growth in demand in SE Asia
1995 War in Saudi Arabia
Major investment in desulphurization plants
Increased shipping costs create premium
1996 Proven oil resources calculations incorrect in Khazakstan
Other fields not economically retrievable in Indonesia
Increased production and refining costs using higher viscosity crudes
1997 OPEC reforms itself

Implications
- Increase demand = higher price
- Loss of supply sources, especially spot market
- Higher refining costs
- Higher inventory costs
- Higher prices
- Pressure for alternative fuels
- Controlled high price

Actions
- Increase distribution facilities
- Purchase oil futures
- Become preferred customer status for shareholders
- Build desulphurization plants
- Review corporate portfolio on investments (alternative fuels manufacturing)
- Create corporate focus on alternate fuels

Scenario 2: Shake-out

Scenario

1995 Global warming increase of 0.5 percent confirmed by EPA

1996 Sadam Hussein invades Kuwait, no Western intervention;
U.S. legislation by 2000 for 5 percent electric cars

1997 UN environmental auto emission standards (sulphur, benzene, aromatics)
Muslim fundamentalists war halts Middle East crude supply
Alternative fuel research booms

1998 Alternative fuel engine made available commercially

2001 Battery-powered Ford Mustang marketed by Japan

Implications

- Reduced product sales
- Asset liquidation by shareholders
- Introduction of cost cutting measures
- Loss of personnel — bronze/paper handshake
- Asset value reduction
- Asset loss — Bahrain refinery

Actions

- Invest in cleaner product
- Invest in product return/recycle
- Streamline business and sell off low-profit assets
- Focus on clean industry fuel supply and advisory services

- Look at technical "brains" assets and align to new business
- Initiate strategic alliance between auto manufacturers and battery developers
- Look for alternate sources of operating and investment funds
- Change operation to alternate fuel supply H2 or methane spurs internal combustion
- Battery exchange or recharge
  Buy technology, manufacture and supply superbatteries

Scenario 3: Boomtown

Scenario

1995 Collapse of oil prices
Poor producing countries flood the market

1996 Greenpeace accused of environmental fraud
Greenhouse effect is a naturally occurring phenomenon

1997 New technology reduces fuel emissions
New strain of sulphur-eating bacteria
Catalytic converters convert exhaust emission to CO_2 and H_2O

1998 Big oil discovery in Sahara

2000 Other alternative fuels still not cost effective

Implications

- High demand/growing markets
- Increased competition/new entrants
- Diversion of investment funds (portfolio review)

Action

- Invest in new, bigger retail sites
- Rationalize old redundant sites
- Upgrade dealer selection process, training, including attendants
- Upgrade retail outlet image
- Advertise promotions
- Improve product quality (R&D)
- Upgrade refineries

Scenario 4: Watch out!

Scenarios

1995 Unforseen global temperature rise
1996 Globally imposed stringent regulation (UN sponsored)
Carbon tax based on exhaust emission
1997 Speed restrictions (50 km/hr) for petro vehicles (USA)
Greenpeace and affiliated pressure groups gain representation in governments
1998 Oil companies seized and proprietary development exposed to public
Global disease linked to petro relation contaminations
1999 High tech communication and travels developed
Super battery car development perfected

Implications

- Negative public pressure/exposure (company seen as "the enemy")
- Requirement for large short-term financing to cover costs of carbon taxes

- More R&D investment
- More diversification investment
- Risk of being nationalized or having assets seized
- Reduction in profit by way of reduced volumes
- Shareholder divestment of the company
- Product segregation by region

Actions

- Invest in environmental R&D, alternative energy companies
- Publicize the above
- Upgrade refineries
- Divest companies considered at high risk of government seizure
- Diversify in different businesses (including alternative energy companies)

Wild Card Scenario

Another, simpler and sometimes revealing approach to writing scenarios is to select a possible "wild card" outcome of a strategic decision, develop a plausible story of how this outcome comes about, and then devise implications and action plans. One group in our multinational oil company example developed a scenario illuminating how the company used desalinated water as a source for fuel by the year 2000.

The scenario in outline form is described below:

Scenario 5: Wild Card

1995 New technology developed to produce hydrogen cheaply and safely from desalinated sea water

1996 Nuclear war in Middle East eliminates oil reserves
Company obtains license to new technology
Mass installation of desalination plants in island countries

1997 Plants constructed in Australia, Philippines, Korea

2000 All world transport powered by hydrogen fuel

Implications
- Company stays in the fuel business
- Major capital investment required for new plant

Actions
- Retrofit existing refineries for desalination/ hydrogen production
- Modify service stations to dispense new fuel
- Construction of desalination plants

Summary

The first example of scenario formulation was an emotionally charged issue. (See Appendix G, L.A. Department of Water and Power.) The best possible turn of events played out under Scenario 2: *What a difference a little time makes.*

The second example illustrates an alternative approach to using scenarios and suggests an all-too-real picture of a future catching up with us before we are prepared, having implications far beyond the telecommunications industry.

These examples show the power of scenarios to break people out of the comfortable mind-set that things will continue as they are and always have been.

CHAPTER THIRTEEN

The Anticipatory Management Process

The Anticipatory Management Process

In this chapter, several tools of Anticipatory Management are combined to present a process for implementation. Remember, the chart in Figure 13.1 crosses divisional lines and departmental boundaries. It involves those individuals who have the most to gain or lose from the impact of an issue.

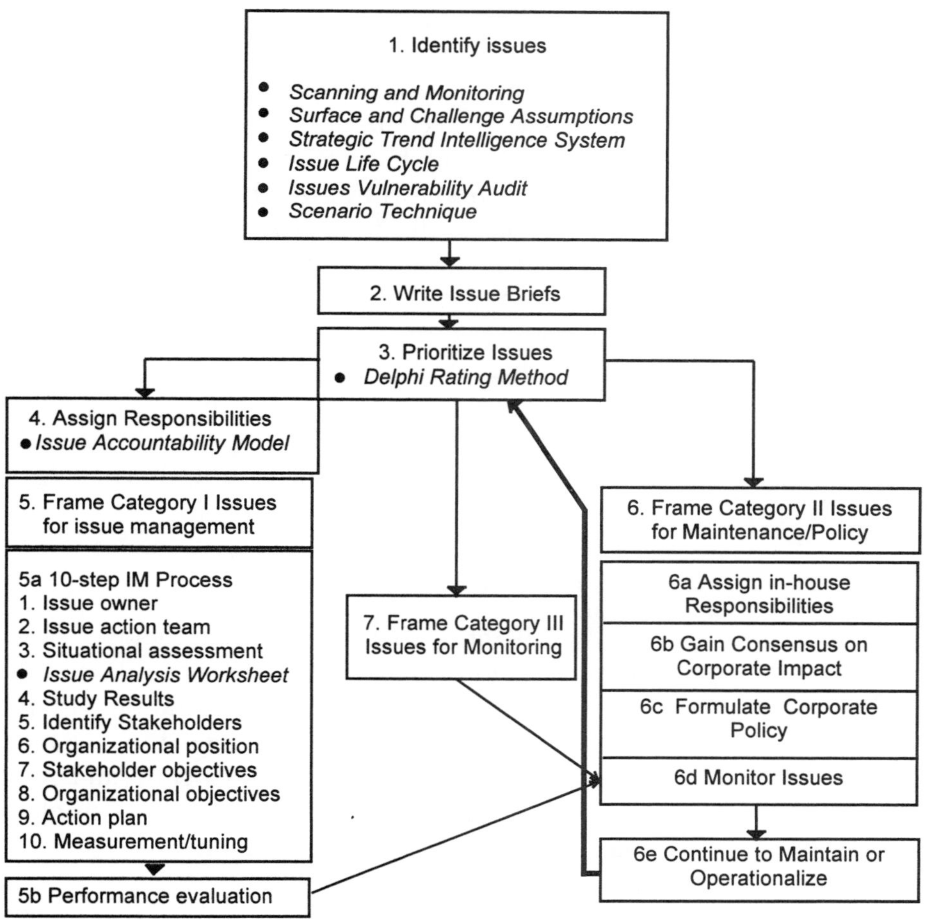

Figure 13.1 Anticipatory management process.

1. Identify issues

Here, we provide raw information for anticipatory management by first working to surface and challenge assumptions (Chapter 3). In addition to scanning, monitoring and forecasting, use the strategic trend intelligence system (Chapter 4). The primary consideration is that trends and events are monitored to ascertain duration, direction, acceleration, and amplitude. As illustrated in the issue life cycle (Chapter 5), *trends* are descriptions of social, technological, economic, environmental, or political (STEEP) movements over time. They define the context within which the organization will function in the future. *Events* are developments that change the future when they occur (e.g., an international free trade agreement). Trends and events converge to form issues like population growth, pollution, and poverty. The issue vulnerability audit (Chapter 6) and the scenario technique (Chapter 12) are also useful in surfacing and challenging assumptions.

2. Write issue briefs

Analysis of the global environment yields a rich quantity of information about issues that could influence the way the organization does business. An issue brief summarizes the issue for management consideration. In general, issue briefs should be no longer than two, single-spaced pages. They should contain:

- A statement of the focus of the issue
- A discussion of its background

- A description of the trends, driving forces, and stakeholders influencing it
- A forecast describing its future prospects
- A listing of potential implications for the organization

See the discussion of a sample issue brief in Chapter 7.

3. Prioritize issues

Sorting issues involves answering several critical questions: What is the probability that the issue will go critical? What is the probability that it will affect the organization? Can the organization influence the issue? Should the organization try? (Chapter 8)

Prioritization categorizes issues into three types:

- Those requiring action (Category I)
- Those that do not require immediate action due to their maturity, their inability to be managed, or their relative unimportance (Category II)
- Those requiring no action (Category III)

Category I issues are discussed according to the 10-step IM model in Chapter 9. Category II issues are too mature in the issue life cycle to manage effectively, but may require organizational policy statements or actions on the part of certain sectors of the organization. Category III issues require no action, but due to their potential impact on the organization, need to be monitored and periodically revisited. The

Delphi Rating Method described in Chapter 8 will help to put priorities on issues.

4. Assign responsibilities

Roles and responsibilities for issues can be determined by applying The Issue Accountability Model (Chapter 10).

5. Frame Category I Issues for issues management

5a. To manage those issues requiring an action plan, refer to the Issue Management Model presented in Chapter 9. Its basic steps are outlined below.

10-step IM process

1. Issue owner
2. Issue action team
3. Situational assessment
4. Study results
5. Stakeholders analysis
6. Organizational position
7. Stakeholder objectives
8. Organizational objectives
9. Action plan implementation
10. Measurement and fine tuning

5b. Performance evaluation

Performance evaluation is the review of the action plan implementation. It assesses how well objectives are attained and how stakeholders respond to the plan. Since the action teams disband once the plan is set in place, performance evaluation is the responsibility of the issues management function.

6. Frame Category II Issues for maintenance and policy

For Category II issues, the emphasis is not on external management and influence but internal containment and compliance.

The organization cannot influence the issue under present circumstances. However, the issue may require an internal structural or policy readjustment to align the organization with the direction in which the issue appears to be headed. The 1992 Americans with Disabilities Act was not something that could be managed immediately; internal policies regarding hiring and architectural adjustments needed to be established.

Such adjustments generally require the involvement of several departments or divisions. Questions must be asked early in the process about which departments will be most affected. Who in the organization has the most information about the issue?

6a. Assign in-house responsibilities

Establishing policy on a mature issue whose full impact is unclear requires the best strategic thinking the organization can muster. This work should not be left entirely to the issues management function, but include those departments most affected.

6b. Gain consensus on corporate impact

At this point in the process, senior management knows that the issue will affect the organization.

Reaching consensus on what, where, and how it will do so requires linking "hard" and "soft" information to strategic thinking.

6c. Formulate corporate policy

Using strategic thinking, the issues management staff and members of affected departments examine the dynamics of the issue from both the outside-in (finding trends and driving forces) and from the inside-out (linking those trends to the operations of the organization). In so doing, the group will identify information needs (e.g., positions within the industry and similarly affected industries).

It is important to remember throughout the issues management process that whereas an issue may be in its emergent stage for one's own organization, it may be much further progressed for another. Someone else may have worked on the issue for a much longer period of time and have valuable information on which to draw. When United Airlines confronted the VDT issue, a check with companies outside the airline industry revealed information that made policy formation much easier.

6d. Issue monitoring

Once the group has done its work, the course to be followed should fall into place. It is important to identify further information needs and charge the issues management staff with monitoring the issue.

6e. Decision to maintain or to operationalize strategic response

Because the future is unpredictable and issues do not always evolve as expected, one must be able to easily move an issue into management mode. Shifts in the environment (social patterns change; economic variables emerge that were not present when a policy was formulated; a new technology surfaces that makes the position less tenable) could lead to a decision that the issue is now a Category I issue. The shift may also be within the organization: a new strategic direction or new product introduction makes the existing policy less valid. The AM model provides for such contingencies.

The AM model emphasizes early identification and analysis of an emerging issue, making use of an issue brief and prioritization rating form. The rating process is essentially an algorithmic decision method. When used, the issue is prepared for strategy, maintenance, and/or policy making. The organization either builds a plan to manage the issue or establishes a position for use throughout the organization and with the various stakeholders.

7. Frame Category III Issues for Monitoring

As discussed earlier, these issues require no action at present. Corporate resources are therefore directed to influence higher priority issues.

Summary

This Anticipatory Management process is a decision support system that systematically links emerging issues to internal decision-making. In the next chapter, we will examine ways of Introducing Anticipatory Management into the Organization.

CHAPTER FOURTEEN

Introducing Anticipatory Management into the Organization

It is pardonable to be defeated, but never to be surprised.

—*Frederick the Great*

While anticipatory management programs may flourish initially, their life expectancy is short without a well-constructed game plan. Great care must be taken when introducing anticipatory issues management to the organization. Machiavelli said it best in the 16th century:

> *There is nothing more difficult to carry out, nor more doubtful of success, nor more dangerous to handle, than to initiate a new order of things. For the reformer has enemies in all those who profit by the old order, and only lukewarm defenders in all those who would profit by the new order, this lukewarmness arising partly from fear of their adversaries, who have the laws in their favor; and partly from the incredulity of mankind, who do not truly believe in anything new until they have actual experience of it.*

How anticipatory management is introduced decides its success. It should be presented as an extension of strategic management, and as a method for discovering forces in the external world which affect decision making at all levels of the company and have bottom-line consequences. It should be presented as decision support, not decision-making, linking the external environment systematically to the internal world of the organization.

Links to Standing Functions

Figure 14.1 demonstrates the relationship of anticipatory management to various standing functions. Since issue management includes ongoing scanning, it can inform colleagues in planning, public affairs, and public relations of emerging issues that may disrupt their work.

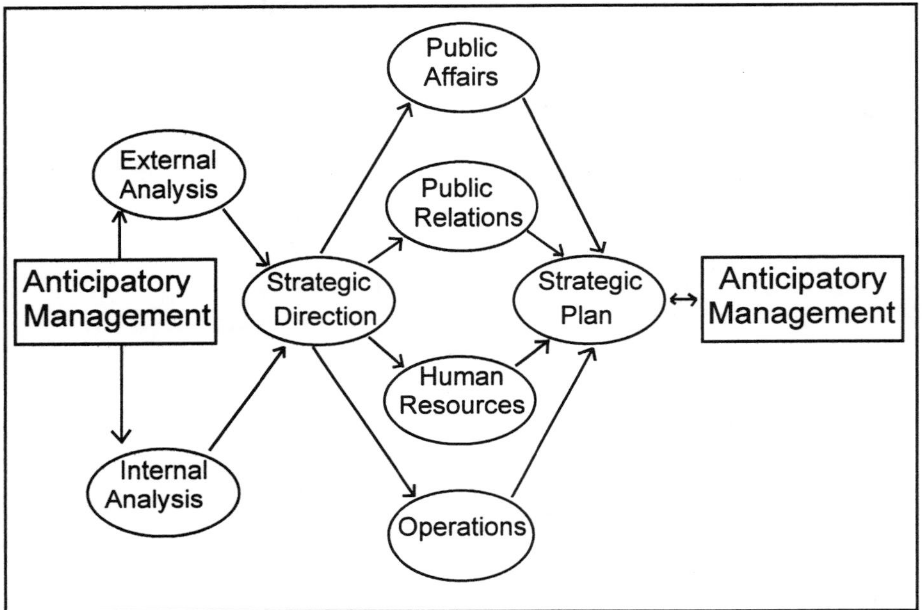

Figure 14.1 Placing anticipatory management within the organization.

Strategic planning

Strategic planning is an exercise in forward-thinking, a disciplined process of attaining specific goals. Its purpose is to best mold the organization to its environment.

Traditional planning uses long-term perspectives to choose a destination and find the best route there. It takes a "snapshot" of the external world as though it were fixed in time. Information is resisted that does not fit the organization's plans of the day. This approach works well through calm times. In turbulent times, it may be disastrous.

Strategic Aikido — the marriage of anticipatory management and planning.

Aikido is the ancient oriental concept that harmonizes the individual with nature. The emphasis is on allowing the individual to balance his or her own needs with those of the environment in which those needs must be met. Anticipatory management offers the organization the opportunity to balance its needs with the needs of society. This is accomplished by providing strategic information in the form of a real-time "motion picture" of the external world. Its ongoing scanning and monitoring functions bring issues (perceived as imbalances with societal expectations) to the attention of the necessary people and assure the opportunity to fine-tune plans.

A rigid organization, like a concrete fortress, is capable of withstanding tremendous force but is devastated by unexpected tremors. The U.S. automobile industry in the '70s is a classic case. Production facilities, organizational structures, product planning, and marketing were based on static conditions. The tremors that rocked the industry were not spontaneous events but foreseeable trends.

Public affairs

Legislation does not inaugurate change; it formalizes change. Public issues can take up to 20 years to be formalized into law.

When issues are addressed by legislation, control is imposed from outside the company. It usually comes with a timetable and a list of conditions with which to comply. Legislation can be very disruptive to an organization if unanticipated, requiring activities outside the current operating budget or strategic plan.

Thoughtful analysis of an emerging issue helps the public affairs unit to be more effective in dealing with stakeholders, to find the lead time to draft position papers and form coalitions, and to reassess existing policies. At United Airlines in 1983, proactive research on the VDT issue helped the anticipatory issues management team write comprehensive testimony for the public affairs people to use in Washington. They had time to take a team of Illinois representatives to visit a reservation center and hear from a radiation specialist before the issue had been raised dramatically in the media.

The lead time United enjoyed on the issue also allowed them to bring in managers from all over the country to share concerns. Ergonomic architects evaluated each reservations center. The work was accomplished on United's timetable and within its normal operating budget.

Public relations

Public relations must integrate diverse perspectives and deal with a wide variety of stakeholders. Some are friendly (e.g., garden clubs or employee groups). Some are neutral (e.g., vendors and service providers). Many are hostile. Consider *60 Minutes'* segment on Food Lion's food quality.

The most effective tool of public relations is quality information. Information about the organization's products and services is generally easy to obtain. Information about the ways products or services are viewed outside the organization is seldom readily available.

In the early '80s, the issues management team at McDonald's Corp. realized that, with 7,000 restaurants and hundreds of suppliers, issues could erupt anywhere and become serious overnight. A 24-hour hotline was established in 1982 so that local managers could reach a PR representative at corporate headquarters at any time. Each representative staffing the hotline was given a book describing the company position on a range of emerging issues.

One major issue was the clearing of rain forests in Latin America. An article in *Life* magazine claimed that McDonald's took advantage of the cleared land to graze cattle cheaply. The public relations team quickly notified special interest groups and other stakeholders of McDonald's beef policies worldwide, including its policy of using only domestic beef in all countries where it operates. Prompt action kept the issue from affecting sales and otherwise interfering with operations.

Industry Institutes and Associations

Organizations often assume that issues are being identified and managed by their association representatives in Washington. This is not always a good assumption. Institutes and associations are evaluated on how well they handle what their members want them to handle, resulting in a kind of reciprocal negligence. If the member companies are not monitoring issues and have not specifically asked their association to manage them, nothing usually gets done.

One of the most serious issues to hit the airline industry in the '80s was the U.S. Department of Transportation's attempt to mandate the use of a jet fuel additive called Avgard for all domestic flights. Avgard alters the molecular structure of fuel from a round molecule whose misting quality allows it to ignite, to a "spaghetti"-shaped molecule that will not burn until the Avgard is removed. Theoretically, this prevents the aircraft from catching fire after a crash.

The issue surfaced when a manager from United Airline's maintenance center in San Francisco brought it to the attention of an action team of line managers investigating cabin safety. When United's public affairs people called the airline association in Washington to find out what the industry position was, they found the association unaware of the initiative. The association's response was that it would wait until the rule was formally proposed and then "shoot it down."

As we saw in the chapter on the issues life cycle, only minor changes can be made once an issue gets to the policy agenda stage, and then only after much weeping, wailing, and expensive lobbying. By acting while the issue was still in the expectations phase, United was able to shift regulators' attention from secondary safety, preventing post-crash fires, to primary safety, avoiding crashes with more sophisticated on-board radar and better use of air traffic controllers.

The Natural Partnership of Anticipatory Management and TQM

Total Quality Management (TQM) is a recent fad for confronting lackluster business results. Many managers are painfully discovering its limitations. Quality improvement is fundamental to removing bad habits, but it is no guarantor of success. A basic flaw exists in the way many companies are applying TQM's concepts of statistical quality control, crossfunctional work teams, empowered work groups, and customer focus. Altering routines is not enough to deal with change. A systematic way of calculating the disruptive impact of change is needed.

Many TQM devotees become mired in methodology. Yet the ability to assess changes that could affect both business and customers is increasingly important. TQM taught organizations something they should have known from the beginning: the customer is important. Anticipatory management teaches that, not only is the customer important, but also that what is important to the customer is important.

Anticipatory management can enhance TQM. As many U.S. manufacturers have learned, doing something properly is still unproductive if it is the wrong thing. Many dilemmas faced in installing TQM are similar to those experienced by strategic planners in the '80s. Many plans failed to anticipate change, so that SWOT (Strengths, Weaknesses, Opportunities and Threats) plans became SPOTS (Strategic Plan On The Shelf).

Anticipatory Management as Part of Something Bigger

In the movie *The Untouchables,* Sean Connery turns to the bad guy who is coming at him with a knife, draws his gun and says, "just like a Dego, showing up for a gunfight with a knife."

Corporate America faces a similar problem: companies are using yesterday's management tools to deal with today's challenges. Managers rely on adversarial argument where someone has to win. They rely on authority to close discussion. They see change as the enemy, disrupting the status quo they are fighting hard to preserve. They are trained to see situations as a series of causes and effects. Events are dealt with individually, with scant attention to the patterns of change which accelerate them.

Functional foxholes

Modern challenges are more complex. The time available to deal with them is shorter, and the penalties are greater than ever. Yet solutions still follow the same formula: break the problem into pieces that fit the present structure and hand out the assignments. The departments or divisions become fiefdoms whose leaders take on the qualities of the six blind men and the elephant from the familiar Sufi tale. Each fiefdom sees the issue from its own perspective and develops solutions from there. The whole picture is never seen.

When one adds the management team concept of high-powered, get-things-done, damn-the-torpedoes, full-speed-ahead leaders, the resolution of issues is further inhibited. Remember that managers' report cards are based on how well their foxholes perform. Much of their effort is focused on gaining or protecting turf and avoiding loss of face.

The winning game

Winning becomes everything. One seeks the enemy within the organization, among stakeholders, even among customers. Most attempts to overcome this enemy mentality are superficial. The management team is put through physically and emotionally challenging games: swinging through trees, fighting paint-ball battles, going white water rafting, fording streams. At best, this treats the symptoms and not the underlying problems. When the team returns to the office, they still have not left their foxholes or escaped the reward systems that reinforce them.

Summary

Anticipatory management has the potential to provide a fresh approach to strategic thinking. It allows the management team to interact meaningfully and non-adversarily outside their foxholes on issues that need not become charged, politicized, or threatening.

CHAPTER FIFTEEN

Solutions to Anticipatory Management Challenges

Current success rates for in-house anticipatory management programs are not high. While many organizations recognize the need for anticipatory management, they go about implementing it the wrong way, or in-house resistance scuttles it.

Many anticipatory management programs are the result of a senior manager attending a meeting or reading an article in the business press. Other programs are begun because an organization has been embarrassed by sales, image, customers, or markets lost over an issue that it should have been aware of, or was aware of but had no action plan.

The reasons for starting an anticipatory management program are less important than the reasons for or the benefits of keeping it viable. A few observations should help the company and its issue manager get off on the right foot.

The Field Theory

"The field is not easily seen from within the field." The Confucian monk who first made this observation some years before Christ could not have had modern American business in mind. Yet, until recently, it was accepted that CEOs and senior managers should come from within the company, or at least from within the industry. Only someone who knew the business intimately could possibly manage it.

When Apple hired John Sculley from Pepsico Inc., it presaged ten years' events that were to follow. Who would have thought that someone from outside the computer industry would be picked to succeed John Akers at IBM?

IBM, with all its resources, and the investment community with all its "informed observers," did not foresee IBM's fate. Perhaps IBM was too deeply inside the field to see the changes on the periphery.

Solution

A major responsibility of the anticipatory management function is to create a strategic trend intelligence system to identify shifts in issues and driving forces that could dislocate the whole industry. The issue manager must become the organization's proponent of outside-in thinking, helping it anticipate change within the field and beyond.

The Lofty Sails Theory

It is not the lofty sails, but the unseen wind that moves the ship.

—W. MacNiele Dixon

Operations, marketing, advertising, training, human resources, public relations, public affairs, and any other divisions are merely the sails of the business. Without the unseen wind from the external environment on which the organization depends for existence, there would be no use for sails. Managers have been trained to perform their functions with little concern for the unseen wind. Their functions are narrowly focused and require intense concentration, preventing even the brightest, most committed manager from catching the breeze. Yet when the ship wanders off course or is becalmed, everyone is held responsible.

Solution

Anticipatory management can assist managers by bringing to their attention external issues that could affect their areas of responsibility and fostering cross-departmental dialogue.

The Boiled Frog Phenomenon

Frogs will, when placed in a beaker of water at room temperature, allow themselves to be boiled to death. Many organizations suffer a similar fate. Everyone interprets all incoming information as reinforcing the organizational direction endorsed by the CEO. Incremental change goes unnoticed. Many organizations are unable to act on conflicting intelligence until too late.

Solution

Managers will attempt to maintain the status quo long after the quo has lost its status. Anticipatory management can ease managers into the changing nature of the world around them through readable issue briefs that present the driving forces — the heat before the water boils — while there is still time to act.

The Monk From the Farthest Temple

One of the most profound frustrations in anticipatory management is the realization of being looked on as "one of them." As an anticipatory manager, it is particularly nice to feel part of the organization since a good part of the work takes one outside of the organization. However, being in-house means being looked on as no smarter than anyone else. Since everyone in the organization is part of the problem, how can the issues manager be part of the solution?

The need arises for someone from outside to help the organization out of its dilemma — "the monk from the farthest temple." The phenomenon was first brought to our attention by a wise Oriental associate after we expressed frustration over the company's hiring of an outside firm to work on issues that had already been addressed. His associate calmly informed us that management only listens to "the monk from the farthest temple."

Solution

Sell the program. Every opportunity must be sought to talk about it, promote its efficacy, involve others, and offer recognition. If that fails, be the first to suggest the need for a "monk from the farthest temple."

The Organization as a Collection of Boutiques

Most divisions within an organization have titles that suggest their function, such as public affairs, public relations, and human resources. The titles give the aura of a boutique where one goes to get specific things done. Boutiques are, by nature, exclusive and sell limited products and services. Unlike department stores, they do not wish to expand their range to meet broad customer needs.

At one time, organizations could exist as a collection of boutiques. Growth was assured and competition minimal. The pie was growing bigger and everyone's slice larger. Human resource problems were handled by human resources (then called personnel). Operations problems were handled by operations, and so on.

Solution

Competition — both domestic and foreign — has increased exponentially. The challenges that were once neat and discrete are now messy, and disrespectful of how the organization is structured. Anticipatory management looks beyond the artificial boundaries of the organization, irrespective of separate boutiques. Individuals are called upon based on proximity and expertise and not what boutique they currently occupy.

The Functional Foxhole Theory of Management

Most current management models were developed in, by, and for industrial organizations. They originated in a template established by the pharaohs of Egypt and were strengthened by successful application in two world wars. The hierarchical methods of these models are based on command and control — the pharaohs, generals, and CEOs had access to information not available to the rank-and-file. Everyone fits into discrete, neatly labeled boxes with rigid production expectations. Each box has an area of responsibility quite different from any other. Any overlap in responsibilities is considered wasteful. Each box becomes very efficient at whatever its "boxness" happens to be.

The model worked well until the late '60s. Then, through careless stewardship, business demonstrated to society that what it did was not always in society's best interests. Discriminatory employment practices, poor product quality, and abuse of the environment shaped societal perceptions. Business discovered that it was not just an economic entity. There were socio-political dimensions to its existence. Almost imperceptibly, but with profound impact, the rules changed. With examples like Sears' equal pay adjustment, issues no longer fit the established boxes. Issues emerged that did not fit any box, but had implications for the entire organization.

In an effort to preserve the organization, boxes became foxholes as the organization declared war with external forces. When the enemy starts shelling, the survival instinct is to dig deeper. For corporate America, this translated into functional foxholes where people become more expert at what they already do. This dig-a-deeper-hole mentality means less communication and more adversarial conduct between boxes.

Solution

Anticipatory management helps the organization manage uncertainty. It positions itself above the foxholes, serving as a military scout, peering over enemy lines, collecting intelligence.

Management by Problem Solving

(Or: If it ain't broke, don't fix it)

Management by problem solving and crisis resolution is a highly unproductive way to run an organization. Solving a problem or resolving a crisis is merely returning the organization to the point it was before the matter arose. Most organizations have completed or are completing a downsizing, de-layering, and resultant demoralizing of their work force in response to external pressures and no-growth markets. Managers are forced to do more with fewer people.

When the issues manager confronts a manager with an other than easily recognizable crisis-proportion issue, the response is invariably, "Buzz off." It is hard to blame the manager, whose rewards and recognition are based on keeping the fires in the attic under control and baling water from the basement. There is little or no reward for plugging leaks or removing potentially combustible material.

Solution

To help sell the program, the senior staff member or issues manager should present anticipatory management as a preventive approach to fires and floods. Examples appearing in Appendix G show how this is done. Anticipatory management can assist managers with additional resources from other areas of the organization to deal with issues before they get out of hand, thereby reflecting badly on the managers and consuming their time. It allows managers to concentrate on innovation and competition, rather than mere problem solving.

Summary

These observations hardly exhaust the solutions to challenges associated with introducing and operating an anticipatory management program. But they should serve as signposts to the issues manager and the organizations that embark down that road.

Bibliography

Aguilar, F. (1967). *Scanning the Business Environment.* New York: Macmillan.

Alinsky, S. (1971). *Rules for Radicals. A Practical Primer for Realistic Radicals.* New York: Random House.

Ansoff, H. I. (1984). *Implanting Strategic Management.* Englewood Cliffs, NJ: Prentice-Hall.

Ansoff, H. I. (1980, April). "Strategic Issue Management." *Strategic Management Journal, 1.*

Ansoff, H. I., Declerck, R. P., & Hayes, R. L. (Eds.). (1976). *From Strategic Planning to Strategic Management.* New York: John Wiley & Sons.

Arrington, C. B., & Sawaya, R. (1984, June). "Managing Public Affairs: Issues Management in an Uncertain Environment." *California Management Review,* 26, 156.

Bartha, P. (1984). "Tuning in on Issues Management". *Canadian Business Review,* 11, 25.

Brown, A., & Weiner, E. (1985). *Supermanaging: How to Harness Change for Personal and Organizational Success.* New York: Mentor.

Brown, J. (1979). *This Business of Issues: Coping with Company's Environments.* New York: Conference Board.

Buchholz, R. A., Evans, W. D., & Wagley, R. A. (1985). *Management Response to Public Issues: Concepts & Cases in Strategy Formulation.* Englewood Cliffs, N.J.: Prentice-Hall.

Chase, H. (1984). *Issue Management: Origins of the Future.* Leesburg, VA: Issue Action Publications.

Choate, P. (1990). *Agents of Influence.* New York: Alfred A. Knoff.

Clarkson, M. B. E. (1993). *The Role and Purpose of Business in Society: The Stakeholder Theory of the Firm.* Toronto, Canada: Center for Corporate Responsibility and Ethics.

Coates, J. F. (1986). *Issues Management: How You Can Plan, Organize and Manage for the Future.* Mt. Airy, MD: Lomond Publications.

Corporate Public Issues and Their Management. Leesburg, VA: Issue Action Publications.

Crable, I. E., & Fibbert, S. L. (1985, June). "Managing Issues and Influencing Public Policy." *Public Relations Review,* 11, 10.

Crossen, Cynthia. (1994). *The Tainted Truth.* New York: Simon & Shuster, 58,59.

Ehling, W. P., & Hesse, M. B. (1983, summer). "Use of 'Issues Management' in Public Relations." *Public Relations Review,* 9, 33.

Ewing, R. P. (1982). "Modeling the Process." J. S. Nagelschmidt (Ed.), *The Public Affairs Handbook,* New York: American Management Association.

Fahey, L., King, W.R., & Narayanan, V.K. (1981). Environmental Scanning and Forecasting in Strategic Planning: The State of the Art. *Long Range Planning, 14(2), 32-39.*

Fahey, L., & Narayanan, V.K. (1986). *Macroenvironmental Analysis for Strategic Management.* New York: West Publishing Company.

Ferguson, D. L. (1986, summer). "Review of Issues Management: Corporate Public Policy-making in an Information Society." *Public Relations Review,* 12, 57-58.

Galvin, R. W. (1991). *The Idea of Ideas.* Schaumburg, IL: Motorola University Press.

Grunig, J. E., & Hunt, T. (1984). *Managing Public Relations.* New York: Holt, Rinehart & Winston.

Hainsworth, B., & Meng, M. (1986). "How Corporations Define Issue Management." *Public Relations Review,* 18-30.

Hanna, N. (1985). "Strategic Planning and Management: A Review of Recent Experiences." (World Bank Working Papers, No. 751). Washington, D.C.: World Bank.

Heath, R. L., & Nelson, R. A. (1986). *Issues Management: Corporate Public Policymaking in an Information Society.* Beverly Hills, CA: Sage Publications.

Johnson, J. (1983). "Issues Management: What are the Issues?" *Business Quarterly,* 48, 24.

Jones, B. L., & Chase, H. (1979, June). "Managing Public Policy Issues." *Public Relations Review,* 5, 3-23.

Magaziner, I., & Patinkin, M. (1989). *The Silent War: Inside the Global Business Battles Shaping America's Future.* New York: Random House.

Makridakis, S. (1990). *Forecasting, Planning and Strategy for the 21st Century.* New York: Macmillan, Inc.

Mintzberg, H. (1994, January-February). "The Fall and Rise of Strategic Planning." *Harvard Business Review.*

McGuire, E. P. (1982). "Public affairs: Its function." J. S. Nagelschmidt (Ed.), *The Public Affairs Handbook,* New York: AMACOM, American Management Association.

Moore, R. (1982). "The evolution of public affairs." J. S. Nagelschmidt (Ed.), *The Public Affairs Handbook,* (pp.9-16). New York: American Management Association.

Morrison, J.L., Renfro, W.L., & Boucher, W.I. (1984). *Futures Research and the Strategic Planning Process: Implications for Higher Education.* ASHE-ERIC Higher Education Report No. 9. Washington, D.C.: Association for the Study of Higher Education.

Nagelschmidt, J.S. (Ed.). (1982). *The Public Affairs Handbook,* New York: American Management Association.

Neufeld, W.P. (1985 September). Environmental Scanning: Its Use in Forecasting Emerging Trends and Issues in Organizations. *Futures Research Quarterly, 1(3), 39-52.*

Schaeberle, R. M. (1982). "Public affairs management." J. S. Nagelschmidt (Ed.), *The Public Affairs Handbook,* (pp. 21-61). New York: American Management Association.

Schaeberle, R. M. (1982). "Public policy." J. S. Nagelschmidt (Ed.), *The Public Affairs Handbook,* (pp. 63-120). New York: American Management Association.

Schaeberle, R. M. (1982). "The state of public affairs." J. S. Nagelschmidt (Ed.), *The Public Affairs Handbook,* (pp. 16-19). New York: American Management Association.

Seitel, F. P. (1987). *The Practice of Public Relations* (3rd ed.). Columbus: Merrill Publishing.

Starling, G. (1980). *The Changing Environment of Business.* Belmont, CA: Wadsworth.

Thompson, D. B. (1981, February). "Issues management: New key to corporate survival." *Industry Week,* 79.

Thorelli, H. B. (Ed.). (1977). *Strategy + Structure = Performance: The strategic planning imperative.* Bloomington, IN: Indiana University Press.

Wilson, I. (1982, August). "Integrating Public Affairs into Strategic Planning." Menlo Park, CA: SRI International.

APPENDIX A

Strategic Trends Defining the Context of the Global Petroleum Industry

The following strategic trends were identified in 1993 by managers in a multinational petroleum company:

- Economic growth in Southeast Asia
- Increased environmental concerns by government
- Reduced investments in mature markets
- Deregulated economies
- Demand for better quality lube-based oils
- Reduction in alternative energy costs, e.g., cheap wind energy
- Population growth in development countries
- Increasingly strict environmental regulations — increased investment cost
- Emerging power blocks
- Increasing deregulation
- Privatization of national oil companies
- High demand in developing countries
- Increasing interest in environmental matters
- Saudi Aramco and other producers going to downsize
- Increased use of alternative energy supply
- Refinery capacity to fall short by year 2000
- New markets opening
- Alternative energy sources becoming more competitive
- Increase in environmental pressures
- Increase in strategic alliances of oil companies and national governments
- Increase in market economies in Latin America and Africa
- Growing population gap between underdeveloped and developed countries
- AIDS increase
- Decreasing political stability

APPENDIX B

Sample Issue Abstract

Title of Article: "How we will work in the year 2000"

Author/Affiliation: Kiechel III, Walter

Publication: *Fortune* Date: May 17, 1993
Pages: 38-52

Summary: By 2000 the average size of U.S. companies will have decreased dramatically. The old blue- collar elite will give way to technical workers who program computers, conduct laboratory tests, or fix copiers. Employees will package themselves as a marketable portfolio of skills. Consequently:

- Businesses will employ fewer people. An average company eliminated 20 percent of its employees over the last 10 years, while tripling its investment in information technology.
- The traditional hierarchies will give way to networked organizations connected to customers and suppliers via electronic channels — virtual corporations.
- Technicians will become the worker elite. Together with professionals (accountants, scientists, and engineers), they will exceed the manufacturing work force.
- The vertical division of labor will be replaced by horizontal division. The important question in the future will not be, "Where do you stand on the corporate ladder?" but, "What do you know how to do?"

- The standard business paradigm will shift from making a product to providing a service — even within what has traditionally been thought of as manufacturing.
- Work will be redefined to involve constant learning, more high-order thinking, and fewer nine-to-five hours. The Internet and related facilities will allow more people to live and work where they want, hooking up electronically to the rest of their organization and working on a project-by-project basis.

Implications: The implication is, business needs to plan to get moving. It needs to plan to move to a more networked "virtual" organization, assisting employees in maintaining and updating their skills. Continuous improvement and keeping up with advances in computer technology, work time scheduling, and electronic commuting need to be stressed.

Monitor's name: John Smith
Title: Vice President Planning

APPENDIX C

Sears Taxonomy (Circa 1976-1981)

From 1976 through 1981, Sears Roebuck & Co. Used the following taxonomy to categorize items identified during scanning and monitoring.

DEMOGRAPHICS

Population

Size and characteristics
- Size
- Growth rate
- Sex
- Age
- Marital status

Births
- Birth expectations
- Fertility rate

Mobility
- Regional
- Metro/non-metro
- Farm
- Central cities
- Congressional districts

Households
- Age of head-of household
- Average size
- One-person households

Minorities
- Illegal aliens
- Spanish Americans

Income

Distribution
- Regional
- Age
- Earners per family
- Education level

Median
- Household
- Individual

Disposable personal income

Spending

Personal consumption expenditures
Consumer price index
Consumer credit

Housing

Existing housing
- units
- type
- region

Housing costs and sales
Housing starts
Incomes of purchasers

Employment

Civilian labor force
Growth rate
Full time, part time
Gender
Working wives
Occupation
Regional distribution
Labor union membership
Hours
Benefits

VALUES AND LIFESTYLES

Values

Public attitudes
Work and leisure
Entitlement
Consumption vs. conservation
Consumer assertiveness

Lifestyles

Marriage and family structure
Homes mobility
Shopping habits
Aging and retirement
Singles

RESOURCES

Energy supply and demand

Coal
Natural gas
Petroleum
Alternative energy sources
- Nuclear
- Solar
- Hydroelectric
- Geothermal
- Photochemical

Industrial Capacity

Research and development

Product development
Manufacturing techniques
Governmental: federal
- Total expenditures
- Defense-related
- Health, Education, and Welfare

Mineral and chemical supply

Imported metals vs. domestic metals

Agriculture

Food
Fertilizer
Agribusiness

Water availability

Supply
- Surface
- Underground

Delivery problem areas
Drought areas

Plastics

Electronic communications

Computers
Networks
Satellites
Entertainment and games

Transportation

People
Materials
Automobiles (electric cars)

PUBLIC AFFAIRS

Consumer confidence

Buying plans index
Consumer credit
Societal attitudes toward:
- Health care
- Government
- Regulations
- Big business
- Corporate social responsibility
- Environment
- Public interest groups
- Consumerism

Governmental operations

Government purchases
Government expenditures
- Welfare
- Social security
- Veterans' benefits
- Employees
- National debt

Economic planning and controls
Government regulations
- Cost
- Criticism
- Reform
- Corporate crimes
- Business lobby

Legislation
- Anti-trust
- Consumerism

Taxes
- Personal
- Corporate
- Social security

Government reports
Economic indicators
Weather modification
Gross national product
- Rate of inflation
- Interest rates
- Unemployment rate
- Productivity
- Bond interest rates
- Capital investment requirements
- Wage levels
- Economic forecasts

Postal service

Environment

Land use
Air, water, and noise pollution
Waste disposal
Weather modification

CORPORATE AFFAIRS

Business

Physical distribution
- Transportation
- Warehousing

Privacy
- Consumer
- Employee
- Corporate

Products
- Safety
- Quality
- Life cycle

Communications with customers
- Advertising
- Marketing
- Complaints
- Warranties

Work place

Physical conditions
Equal opportunity
Benefits
Job security

INTERNATIONAL AFFAIRS

World population

5,000,000,000 people
Doubling period
Birth control

Global resources

Food
Energy
- Known reserves
- Political stability

Raw materials
Trade
- Payment balance
- Exports
- Imports
- Protectionism
- Tariffs
- Cartels

Developing nations

OPEC
Less-developed countries (LDCs)
Technology transfer

APPENDIX D

Issue Vulnerability Audit Results

The following list of organizational strengths and vulnerabilities were generated when a group of multinational corporate petroleum executives applied the Issues Vulnerability Audit to their work.

Case Example

NEEDS AND WANTS

STRENGTHS	VULNERABILITIES
Diversified location	Threat of nationalization
Electricity generation	Cheaper and safer energy sources become available
Compressed natural gas	Depleted supply
Petroleum products	Medical evidence showing petroleum products harmful
Multi-markets	World economic recession
Shipping/distribution	Pollution; Government regulation
Transportation	Technology reduces vehicle use
Crude exploration	Low crude prices
Service stations	High costs; Environmental issues
Oil	Recycling of waste oil
High product quality	Alternative supply source
Quality/service at retail outlet	Self-service
Market strength	Scandal
Corporate image	Potential Oil spill
Trading	Elimination of middle men
Multinational company	Wide scale nationalization
Shipping	Pipeline networks
Large scale gasoline supplier	High efficiency gasoline engine

CUSTOMER BASE

STRENGTHS	VULNERABILITIES
Coal	Depletion of reserve
Do-it-yourself Lubes	Gov't. regulation on pollution
Shipping	Economic depression
Agriculture	Flood, drought

Strengths (continued)	**Vulnerabilities (continued)**
Retail customers	Shift in base, inadequate investment
Governments of dev countries	Regulation
Power plants	Alternate source products
Crude buyers	Conflict areas, uncertain supplies, coal degasification
Quality-conscious customers	Grudge purchasing
Airlines	Higher quality specifications
Mining industry	Low emission fuel Water-based fluids
Industrial plants	Conversion to pneumatic controls Co-generation
Retail outlets	New design and facilities from competition
Farming	Changing agricultural practices
Airlines, jet fuel	Increased efficiency reduces demand
Growing customer in SE Asia —	China reverts, growth slows because of lack of Infrastructure
Petrochemical products use naphtha	Gas replaces
Trucking fleets	Fuel efficient engines Alternate mode of transport
Generating plants	Alternative fuel — wind, coal, nuclear
Motor cycles	Environmental concern with smoke Personal hazard
Government, public transport	Wide scale change to electric busses & trains
Road constructors	Greater use of concrete or other synthetics

APPENDIX E

Sample Issue Brief

Sample Issue Brief

Energy Crisis in the '90s

Issue focus

Despite the oil glut, indications are that the U.S. could be moving toward another energy crisis. In the face of danger signs, is the company taking adequate precautions against the possibility of escalating fuel prices or another OPEC-induced price shock?

Background

After rising from $3.25 per barrel in early 1973, to $34 in late 1981, the recent price slump has created complacency over U.S. energy supplies and made OPEC seem irrelevant. Following several years of decline, energy consumption is rising again with the economic recovery. The current energy surplus may be temporary. Oil prices are likely to rise during the '90s, while American dependence on Middle Eastern oil may lead to new shortages and supply interruptions.

Driving forces

The current energy surplus could create problems for the future. Faced with a huge price slump and the threat of hostile takeovers, American oil companies have closed 140 refineries since 1981, reduced the number of operational drilling rigs from more than 4,000 to 1,850, and cut back on exploration. Because of long lead times, lack of exploration now could mean shortages in the next decade. Consumption rises, because low prices discourage conservation and investment in alternative energy technologies.

The increase in known reserves has slowed dramatically. Global reserves have increased only five percent since the mid-'70s, compared to 900 percent between 1950 and 1973. Within 15 years, the reserves of major non-OPEC oil producers — the U.K., Mexico, and the U.S. — may be nearly exhausted.

Future prospects

The International Energy Agency in its World Energy Outlook has stated that the world will grow ever-more reliant on Middle Eastern oil. They forecast that the OPEC oil nations are likely to provide nearly half the world's oil supply by the year 2010, up from 30 percent today. While oil prices are expected to fall in the short term, prices could rise to $35-$54 per barrel by the late '90s (discounting inflation). High crude oil prices might last a decade until alternative fuels begin to replace oil. The Middle East is likely to remain politically unstable and may ignite a major power conflict.

Increasing domestic exploration or cutting use could provide some protection. Proposals have been made to tax imported oil, raise taxes on gasoline, introduce a more general carbon tax, maintain the Strategic Petroleum Reserve, pursue synthetic fuel demonstration projects and impose more stringent conservation standards. Government has urged industry to move away from petroleum fuels and prepare for a costly energy environment.

There is limited political support for measures that would restrict energy consumption and increase government expenditures. The Department of Transportation is rolling back the Corporate Average Fuel Economy (CAFE) standards imposed on auto manufacturers in the '70s. A tax on fuel imports could prove an attractive remedy for the $300 billion federal deficit.

Implications

The sharp rise in fuel prices following the OPEC oil embargo and the Iranian revolution in 1979, placed a severe strain on many air carriers, and the lack of fuel in some locations brought government intervention. The company is negotiating new long-term contracts with its fuel suppliers. Fuel efficiency is weighed in aircraft acquisition plans. Given warnings about energy shortages, should any plans be modified? A number of proposals are being floated to help protect the nation's energy supplies. Could the company benefit from more active participation in shaping future energy policy?

APPENDIX F

Sample Delphi Issue Rating Sheet and Consensus Report

Sample Delphi Issue Rating Sheet and Consensus Report

Energy Crisis in the '90s

Name: ____________________

Issue Focus

Despite the oil glut, indications are that the U.S. will face rising prices and potentially risky dependence on Middle Eastern oil a decade from now.

Stage of Development

Place the issue at the appropriate point on the time line below.

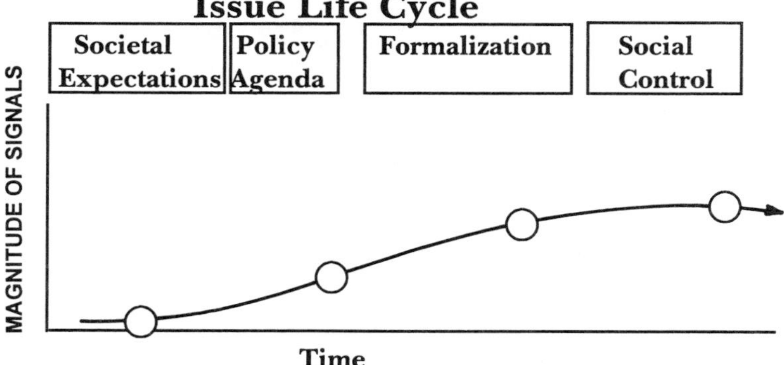

Issue Evaluation

To what extent *can* the company influence the direction and nature of this issue, if it starts now?

-2	-1	0	+1	+2
We really can't do anything to affect the issue.		I'm not certain.	If we begin now, we will have the widest array of options.	

To what extent *should* a company address this issue?

-2	-1	0	+1	+2
This issue is irrelevant. The company should ignore it.		I'm not certain.		We would be negligent not to address this issue.

Priority Assignment

Indicate your position whether the organization *can* or *should* address the issue.

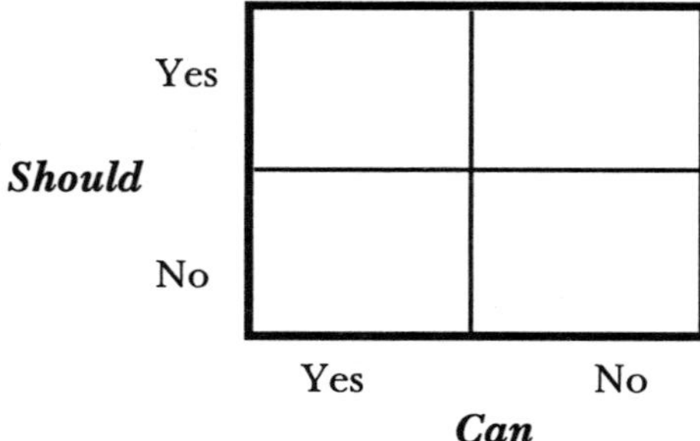

Degree of Familiarity

Indicate your familiarity with this issue by circling one of the marks.

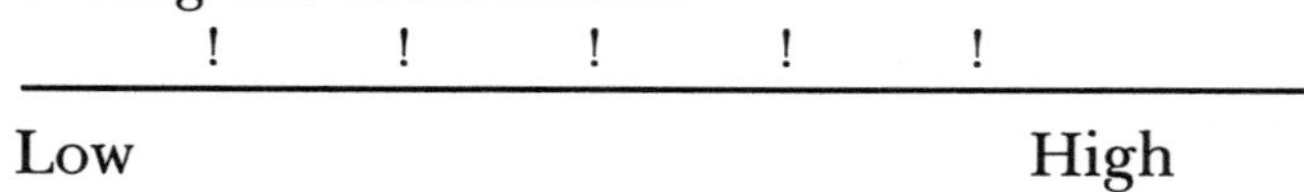

Additional Observations

Please use the reverse side to raise questions about or comment on the nature, direction, and management of this issue.

Sample Consensus Report

This report summarizes the results of individual Delphi Rating Sheets with responses indicated by managers' initials.

Issue Focus

Despite the oil glut, indications are that the U.S. will face rising prices and potentially risky dependence on Middle Eastern oil a decade from now.

Stage of Development

Place the issue at the appropriate point on the time line below.

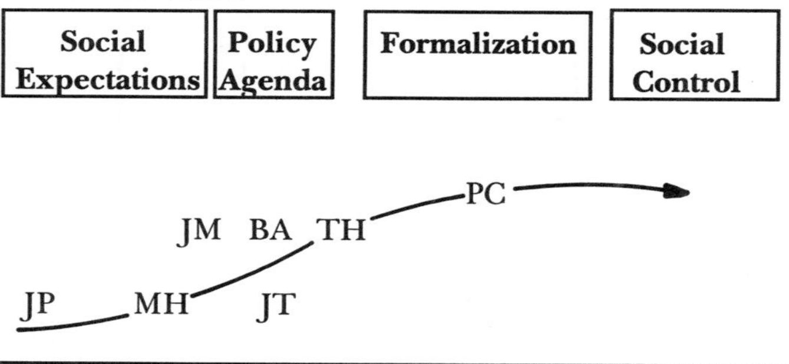

Time

Issue Evaluation

To what extent can the company influence the direction and nature of this issue if it starts now?

MH

PC JP TH JT BA JM +2

We really can't do anything to affect the issue.	I'm not certain.	If we begin now, we have the widest array of options.

To what extent should the company address this issue?

JT
JP TH PC MH +1 JM BA

This issue is irrelevant. The company should ignore it. — I'm not certain — We would be negligent not to address this issue.

Priority Assignment

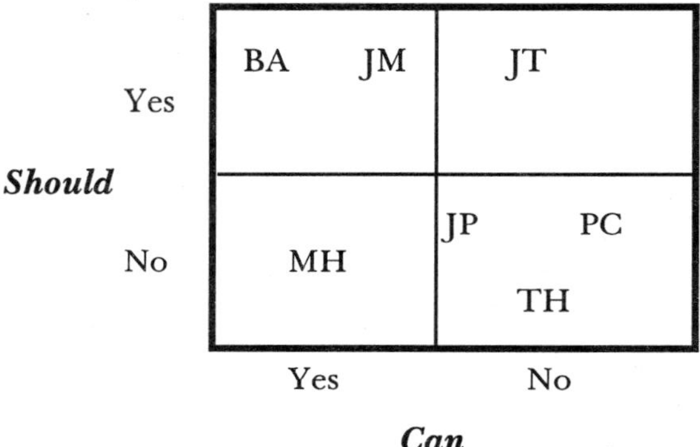

Degree of Familiarity

Indicate your familiarity with this issue by circling one of the marks.

PC JP
! ! MH TH JT JM BA

Low High

APPENDIX G

Case Studies: Issues Management in Action

L.A. Department of Water and Power: Air Quality

In April 1989, a meeting was held of the senior managers who comprised the executive committee of the Los Angeles Department of Water and Power (DWP). Among the top subjects selected that day for the pilot issues management effort was air quality. Although this issue was not new to the DWP, it was one which was perpetually emerging in several costly dimensions and required a continuous creative response on the part of the utility's management.

The air quality issue was identified as belonging to the power system, whose chief executive named the engineer in charge of the System Development Division as the issue's logical owner. The System Development Division is responsible for relations with regulatory agencies and development of plans for emissions reductions.

Rule 1135

In May 1990, while the issues management air quality action team was busy putting together its issues management model, the South Coast Air Quality Management District (SCAQMD) in California was asking utilities for compliance plans to meet specifications of Rule 1135.

Rule 1135 covered the reduction of various emissions from stationary sources to meet specific air standards. The costs could run the utilities as much as $1 billion each during the 1990s, with a projected deadline of seven years to retrofit facilities to meet the new guidelines.

Various technologies were available, but the SCAQMD favored an add-on retrofit process. The utilities were opposed because of the additional stress on existing facilities with no long-term benefits. The familiar confrontational mode was in the works, with the SCAQMD politically the champion of "clean air" and the utilities appearing recalcitrant about costs and time schedules.

A different response

The issues management action team quickly began meetings to draft their response. Although aware of the cost and scheduling arguments, they looked closer at all the environmental ramifications of the two choices. The action team noted that repowering helped mitigate both local ambient air conditions and the Greenhouse Effect, while retrofitting actually added to the potential Greenhouse Effect.

Starting off with an introduction that vowed full support for the goals of the SCAQMD, the team's response did not touch on monetary issues, but instead, zeroed in on the positive environmental effects of repowering and the dramatic savings in fuel costs. Now the response dealt with the environment exclusively and not a clash of values. Also, the repowering process would take ten instead of seven years, giving the utility more time to work out solutions.

It was now up to the chief executive of the power system to decide which approach to use: the traditional response or the action team's response. At first he was amused by the two different approaches. He decided to go with the action team's approach, and a formal response was prepared, declaring the utility's cooperative position and advocating the best possible solution to a jointly recognized air quality problem.

A successful gamble

The gamble had been taken. By now, the staff had become comfortable with the action team's approach, and endorsement was internally unanimous without any coercion from the chief executive. The next step was to test the suggestion with the SCAQMD. Even though the utility had compelling reasons to support its approach, it was still asking for ten years instead of seven. Would the SCAQMD like the re-powering method well enough to wait patiently for three more years?

In May 1990, the utility's Emission Control Plan for Rule 1135 was submitted to the SCAQMD. Conditioned to the debate format with which such matters were usually approached, the commission was pleasantly surprised by the cooperative tone of the document.

At first, the SCAQMD considered only the negative aspect of extending compliance three more years. Staff review of the repowering option soon effected a turn-around, and the SCAQMD praised the utility for bringing the ramifications of retrofitting to the SCAQMD's attention. The utility had made itself part of the solution rather than part of the problem. The

SCAQMD staff felt more comfortable in their relationship with the utility.

The issues management action team was free to pursue their air quality action plan without the fallout that might have resulted from Rule 1135. The team had proven their worth, and the issues management process had proven its benefits in a very short time. Issues management teams working in other areas found strong encouragement for their work. Management was pleased to have initiated the process, and other area utilities became interested in creating their own issues management programs.

Beyond the intangible benefits of an established issues management process and the personal gratification for all who took part in the action team, lay the financial benefits. Although other savings were expected in the years ahead, the utility had already experienced an estimated $100 million in fuel savings with the approval of the repowering option.

Sears, Roebuck and Co.: Regulation of Interstate Commerce

The history of commerce regulation dates to the passage of the Act to Regulate Commerce and the establishment of the Interstate Commerce Commission (ICC) in 1887. Although the legislation has been amended many times, the public utility-type regulation of the common-carrier industry continued until recently. The ICC had far-reaching jurisdiction over pricing, mergers, abandonments, and service.

A new level of commitment

The campaign for motor carrier regulatory reform was planned more painstakingly than any other Sears public policy. It required a cooperative effort around four principal goals:

- Organizing a coalition
- Supporting the administration's initiative
- Establishing "grass roots" legislative contacts
- Drafting corporate position statements and publicizing them

An inefficient transportation system

After World War II, American society and Sears went through important changes as problems presented opportunities for growth. An expanded highway system offered opportunity for movement. Society did move, and Sears followed, shifting retail into high gear with a greater reliance on trucking.

The media heightened public awareness of the inefficiency inherent in a regulated industry. Documentaries, magazine articles, editorials, and publications from business "think tanks" such as the American Enterprise Institute portrayed the restraining effects of regulation and the burden they placed on the common-carrier segment of the transportation industry. The shipper and the consuming public had to pay the costs, running into the billions of dollars per year. The attention produced a call for prompt and decisive action.

The physical distribution department at Sears was established in 1971 as a result of its awareness of the problem. The Washington office became involved; corporate leaders took the initiative by writing to the president.

Early moves toward deregulation

As far back as 1954, organizations to study the transportation problem were established when President Eisenhower created a committee under the guidance of Secretary of Commerce Sinclair Meeks. In his words, "The vital interests of the nation require that the transportation industry of the United States maintain itself at maximum effectiveness."

Meeks' recommendations to Eisenhower included greater reliance on competition in transportation pricing, and reduction of regulation to a minimum. Yet it was not until 1966 that the Department of Transportation was established by then-president Johnson. By that time, retail associations, as well as Ralph Nader's group, were pushing transportation regulatory reform. In 1971, a group of 12 major corporations established the Committee on Modern Efficient Transportation (COMET) to support the Nixon administration's moves toward deregulation.

Sears actively supported COMET and its newsletter. It arranged transportation blitzes using local store managers. Its Washington office set up conferences to explore the issue's parameters. In 1978, Sears' Governmental Affairs office created a file of editorials from publications across the country, which proved helpful in pressing for decontrol on Capitol Hill.

Slow congressional response

Proposals were submitted to Congress and placed on the agenda, receiving considerable attention, review, and study, but producing little action. Hearings were held in the 94th and 95th congresses. Still, it was not until 1976 that President Ford signed an omnibus rail bill, which effectively left reform to the ICC. In 1980, the Staggers Railway Improvement Act was passed, leading to an explosion in the number of short lines able to profit where larger companies could not.

Sears came out strongly for transportation regulatory reform, as evidenced by the company's chairman, Robert E. Wood's letter to President Ford. George Tidmarsh spoke of the need for new directions in transportation. The Washington office presented Sears' views to legislators. By mid-1970, Sears adopted formal policies on transportation. The Motor Carrier Reform Act passed in mid-1980. Reporting on the campaign, Stan Sender, Sears chief lobbyist on the issue, said:

"Our victory, while substantial, was very close. The Sears store managers' efforts in writing twice to Senate Commerce Committee members and George Tidmarsh's personal lobbying efforts on the Hill played an important part in the grass-roots effort which gave us a narrow edge of success."

Cost savings

Decontrol spelled opportunity. The bottom line deeply affects society and Sears in terms of freedom, flexibility, and one-to-one negotiations. At Sears, it means maximizing the use of existing terminal systems and lowering unit costs — a 10 percent savings on distribution, and considerably less hassle.

Although the system for dealing with strategic public issues in the "Challenge Decade" emphasized the restraining impact of control, the program discussed demonstrates that with the new administration's attitude, regulation can effectively be used to foster decontrol as well.

Boeing Corp.

In 1992, Boeing instituted an issues management process under the auspices of Corporate Government Affairs to identify, understand, and manage federal government issues that affect the company. The process is described below.

Issue identification

An issue may be identified by any one of the main Boeing divisions or by corporate staff.

Corporate Government Affairs reviews each issue to determine whether to expend company resources on the issue. If so, an issue manager and a team are assigned to the issue. Government Affairs and the issue team decide the issue's priority, based on an established set of criteria.

Issue approval

Once an issue is identified and prioritized, the team drafts a 1-3 page white paper describing the issue, its background, its implications, and the company's objectives. The white paper is circulated for approval by the legal department and public relations before being sent for final approval by the Corporate Executive Council.

Working an issue

Upon final approval by the Executive Council, the issue formally becomes part of the issues management system. It is logged in a computer database together with the white paper, the issue team make-up, and an overview. The database is accessible to Government Affairs staff both in Seattle and Washington, DC. The Washington staff, working with the issue manager and the issue team, decides how to achieve a successful resolution of issues and provides status reports via the database.

When an issue has been resolved successfully or no longer affects the company, it is dropped from the issues list and archived.

Priority definitions

Critical issues: Favorable resolution of these issues is necessary to achieve the corporate long-range goals and objectives. The existence of the corporation, division, or project could be jeopardized.

Important issues: Unfavorable resolution of these issues would make it difficult to meet one or more of the long-range goals or objectives. The financial impact is expected to be measured in billions of dollars.

Significant issues: The outcome could be of significance to the corporation. Expending resources to achieve a favorable outcome will have some likely benefit. The financial impact is expected to be measured in millions of dollars.

Monitor—of interest: These issues lack definition, or the degree of activity around them is uncertain. They could move to the priority list if the issue is taken up by relevant committees of Congress or the Executive Branch or if the company interest becomes better defined.

General Comments

The issue management process has worked reasonably well in helping the company become proactive on external issues that directly or indirectly affect its operations. White papers help to articulate an issue's importance and restate company objectives. Some issues remain nevertheless, ill-defined, and sometimes it is difficult to distinguish the real from the spurious.

Georgia Power Company

This description of issues management at Georgia Power Company was written in 1994 by James Vaseff, manager, external issues.

Role and goals

The role of the external-affairs issues identification committee of Georgia Power is to give management intelligence on issues, not more information. The process described is issue and action oriented; the committee is not to be seen as a detached think tank.

Wherever possible, issues should be linked to competitive concerns and GPC's bottom line. Numbers, comparative scales, and so on can be used to describe savings or losses related to issues. It must be possible for issues to move through the company for this work to have a positive effect. The place this starts is in the committee. Various experts are brought in on different issues to get them, as prime sources of information, to buy into the process.

To keep long-term credibility, the committee is to be regarded as a purveyor of insight and information, not an issues advocate. The successful implementation of ideas from the committee will come from the understanding and adoption of those ideas by management or departments that see the information as important to their operations.

Sometimes the crystal ball is clearer to one reader than others. Sometimes ideas, for good or bad reasons, die after a fight. The committee, if it is to operate over the long run, must stay above the fray and be seen as a neutral player.

Output from the committee is to be in a consistent format, so that people can expect information in a certain form. A formal process gives the committee's work a "signature," much like a magazine or newscast, that people are comfortable with—the better to comprehend the issues being discussed.

A process for issues management

Presently GPC has many issues in various stages of study and management. Acid rain, EMF, and solid waste are examples. The available body of information can accelerate the issues management process; there is no need to start cold. The formal process of issues identification has three major steps: issue identification, issue framing, and stakeholder analysis.

Issue Identification

This is a structured brainstorming session that directly and indirectly identifies issues. Each idea brought up is subjected to a process called the "Implications Wheel." The implications of each idea are documented in four categories *(social, technological, economic, and political).* The results of each of these categories are again subjected to the Implications Wheel. Graphically, this exercise looks like a chain reaction. The Implications Wheel verifies known issues and discovers related issues that were not thought of before.

Issue framing

Issue framing develops a clear, unbiased description of an issue. It should involve:

- A definition of the issue
- Driving forces behind the issue
- Likely outcomes
- Implications for the industry
- Threats
- Opportunities
- Challenges for the company

These categories are investigated by the committee and then drafted by a single author for review and verification. An issues paper is developed.

Stakeholder analysis

This is where an action plan is developed. Stakeholder analysis determines which groups will have an interest in an issue and weighs their interest and effect on it. This information is used to build a matrix whereby each stakeholder's involvement and position on the issue can be categorized. From the matrix, the committee develops an action plan for education and other activities.

Time demands on the committee

The committee establishes its work schedule after determining the number of issues to deal with, getting familiar with the energy needed for each of the three steps in the process, and producing a work plan. Most, if not all, immediate issues can be identified and processed in one session of the committee.

National Cattlemen's Association

Lisa Forst, director, issues management for the National Cattlemen's Association provided the following description of their process in 1993.

Managing issues for success

Two essentials are necessary for any industry to sustain long-term profitability. One is a friendly business climate, and the other is a marketplace receptive to the industry's product at a price that is profitable. These essentials must never be separated. To invest heavily in one while ignoring the other is to live in a fool's paradise.

The nuclear power industry would certainly agree. There is robust demand for its product (electricity), but the business climate is so bad that power plants are being closed and dismantled. Over-regulation by the government and negative public image will ultimately drive the profit from any industry despite all efforts to sustain it.

Maintaining a friendly business climate and receptive marketplace must be a deliberate and clearly defined priority for any industry. Simply running one's business—even if done well—while hoping the business climate will remain friendly amounts to wishful thinking. Malcolm Forbes described wishful thinking as a contradiction in terms. It is, indeed.

The National Cattlemen's Association (NCA) works to maintain a friendly business environment for cattle producers and a receptive marketplace for beef through a comprehensive process called *issues management.* To truly manage issues, one cannot wait until the media calls for a statement and then hope to be quoted correctly in the newspaper. To manage issues is to participate in the process by which the issues are defined, resolved, and communicated to the public. Issues don't fall from the sky. They evolve. To manage them, one must be part of the process from Day One.

The issues management process employed by the NCA includes eight components:

- **Policy formation**

  The cornerstone of the NCA's issues management process is industry policy developed through a grass-roots system that involves cattlemen, not staff or consultants, making policy decisions. Without clear policy, neither NCA nor anyone else can serve the interests of cattlemen.

- **Government affairs**

  Many of the issues important to cattlemen are based on government legislation or regulation. Issues management must include a way to influence government decisions. NCA uses the most powerful government affairs tool available: grass-roots lobbying. By maintaining a professional staff presence in Washington, DC, the NCA is involved from Day One in important issues--long before issues are fully defined.

- **Public relations**

  If stakeholders, such as the media, government regulatory agency personnel, and mainstream public interest groups are kept in the dark about the cattle industry, they are likely to accept myths about it. As gatekeepers, these stakeholders can either let information reach the consumer or not. An effective public relations program closes the gate to myths and opens it to facts.

- **Producer awareness and involvement**

  Since many of the issues that confront the industry pertain to the on-site practices of cattlemen (environmental management, animal drug use, excess fat production, etc.), cattlemen must participate in resolving issues at the farm, ranch and feed-lot level. The NCA and its affiliates have unmatched capabilities to get the word to cattlemen on actions to take at the local level in resolving an issue.

- **Research and intelligence**

  Effective issues management requires that issues be identified long before they enter the public domain. Understanding the underlying trends is essential if issues—especially explosive ones—are to be resolved in a way favorable to cattlemen. The NCA has developed an extensive network that gives it access to information in the formative stages of issues.

- **Experts and coalitions**

  Many of the issues that the NCA deals with are highly technical: food safety, the environment, health and diet, and so on. The NCA uses a network of third-party experts to analyze the scientific aspects of an issue before its members set policy on it, so that cattlemen can make informed decisions. The NCA's network of contacts allows the formation of coalitions to confront issues the NCA cannot win alone.

- **Industry initiatives**

  Issues cannot be resolved with lip service. Action is needed to demonstrate that the industry is working in concert with the public interest. The "war on fat" is a good example. After years of frustration and negative publicity about dietary fat, the beef industry did something—by trimming excess external fat. The industry changed the product in the eyes of consumers. As a result, consumer attitudes about the leanness of beef have steadily improved.

  The Beef Quality Assurance program is another example. Negative publicity about animal drugs has virtually disappeared, as has the problem with injection-site blemishes.

- **Partner communications**

  Cattlemen are not the only ones affected by the business climate for beef. Those with investments in auction markets, packing plants, restaurants, grocery stores, and so on also have a vested interest. The NCA has stepped up communications with these stakeholders so that they may feel comfortable that issues are being managed effectively. The degree to which they promote and market beef is affected by the degree of comfort they have in the beef industry's future.

The loss of public confidence in private industry creates a climate for costly government intervention or outright discrimination against products. Traditional public relations has proven unsuccessful as a defense against eroding public confidence and deteriorating business climate. The NCA has implemented an issues management program that goes far beyond the norm, and it is proving to be effective.

Weyerhaeuser Company

This program description was prepared by Gary O'Malley, director, issue management, in 1994.

Weyerhaeuser is highly visible in many communities nationwide. It is one of the largest private owners of timberland in the country, with almost Six million acres and operations in 43 states. The issues Weyerhaeuser faces generate significant public interest, and the number and complexity of those issues can only increase.

Sometimes, we learn the facts at work. More often, though, we're unfamiliar with the legislative and public-policy decisions that affect our livelihoods. Critical decisions threaten to make past and future forestry investments uneconomical, prohibit the marketing of products to certain markets, or close mills on environmental technicalities.

At stake are hundreds of millions of dollars annually. The company's profitability is on the line, and that translates into a potential loss of money or raises, benefits, new equipment for the mill or office, and professional-development opportunities.

Accurate and timely information is critical to the corporation, if it is to manage successfully the issues that challenge it, both to minimize their negative impact and to realize potential advantages. As a company, Weyerhaeuser needs to change to meet the times. The times require that it does a better job of informing employees and other audiences on issues of importance.

The issue management process

To address its most pressing issues, Weyerhaeuser has established an issue management process that provides a structured means of identifying emerging issues early enough to influence public opinion. It ensures that the public, including its employees, is accurately informed; and it ensures effective deployment of limited company resources.

How issues are identified

"Candidate" issues are defined as "any matter of public interest or concern that involves specific and identifiable public (including employee) or government action that can significantly benefit or harm Weyerhaeuser."

The issues that can be most costly—or most helpful—to Weyerhauser's business or its core values are those to focus on. Weyerhaeuser wants to make sure it expends resources on issues that it can influence uniquely with a high likelihood of success.

Impending changes to current issues or the emergence of new issues are brought to light through a variety of sources: concerned business managers, issue managers, government affairs personnel, employees, and senior management. Issue managers—usually senior business or staff managers—work with the appropriate company divisions to establish priorities and strategies, including active participation by senior management in determining company involvement.

How issues are classified

- **Class I**: Active issues having a high beneficial or negative impact on the company volatile, internally sensitive, a priority for senior management
- **Class II:** Active issues having a high beneficial or negative impact; potentially volatile or internally sensitive, priority for concerned business or staff managers
- **Class III:** Fading, dormant or emerging issues that have potentially high impact; monitor only
- **Class IV:** Issues that may have a very significant impact. External Affairs Councils, composed of senior business and staff managers in each state, manage these issues

Once issues are identified, they are prioritized to help focus time and energy. Active issues involving Weyerhaeuser core businesses and having a high impact on the company's short- and long-term profitability are identified as Class I.

Examples

The wetlands issue in the South and the spotted owl issue in the Northwest are Class I issues.

- In North Carolina, the wetlands issue challenges Weyerhaeuser ability to practice normal silviculture on hundreds of thousands of acres.
- In the Northwest, the decision to include private land in regulation of the spotted owl's habitat threatens Weyerhaeuser's ability to manage and harvest more than 250,000 acres of timberlands.

Issues with potential for high impact yet generally limited to individual businesses, or having less severe results to the company, are listed as Class II.

Fading, dormant, or emerging issues are considered Class III, needing monitoring only; while Class IV issues are those with potentially significant impact but which are limited in scope to a particular state. The issues change quickly. Sudden public or legislative attention can propel issues from anonymity to critical status overnight. The new issues management process helps identify changes quickly and prepare appropriate responses to new issues. Conversely, it requires that Weyerhaeuser "pull the plug" on issues that no longer require aggressive attention.

How employees will be involved

Communication is central to the issues management process. Through *Weyerhaeuser Today, Management Bulletin,* employee forums, issue summaries, and other means, Weyerhaeuser hopes to keep employees continuously updated on current issues and the positions the company has taken. Weyerhaeuser is currently evaluating the merits of establishing a toll-free number for employees to get facts about issues important to the company.

The benefits of issues management

It's a simple fact: Public policy decisions have great impact on Weyerhaeuser's bottom line. Weyerhaeuser can dramatically affect its profitability by managing issues responsibly and consistently. Through its involvement in the Oklahoma Wilderness Bill, the company helped secure an amendment allowing the U.S. Forest Service to acquire Weyerhaeuser lands outside the national forest boundary. The amendment could consolidate up to 140,000 acres of company land and ensure compensation of tens of millions of dollars.

The issue team handling the Clean Air Act worked with a congressman from Washington state whose position was pivotal to delete industrial boilers from the act, saving the company $20 to $50 million annually.

The issue management process:

- Focuses resources on a few vital issues.
- Ties resources directly to corporate goals, values, and business strategies.
- Ensures that the company sets clear objectives and assigns accountability for meeting them.

By following a clearly defined process, a unified Weyerhaeuser can speak with one voice on high-priority issues.

INDEX

A.H. Robins, 137
ABI Inform, 75, 134
Across the Board, 73
Adams, John, 13
Aguilar, Francis, 60, 63
Air quality, 172-177, 118, 119, 261-264
Airline industry, 6-7, 206
Airplane cabin safety, 132, 134
Akers, John, 39, 108, 213
Alar, 83-84, 96
Alinsky, Saul, 137
Allstate Insurance Company, 72
American Demographics, 73
American Enterprise Institute, 75
American Council of Life Insurance, 73
American Telephone & Telegraph, 71, 91, 115
Apple Computer, 213
Assumptions, surfacing, 45-55
Atlantic, 73
Audubon Society, The, 74
Automobile industry, 8-9, 49-50, 203
Avgard, 132, 206

Bankruptcy reform, 115
Barratt Development, PLC, 52-53
Bibliolinks, 76
Boeing Corporation, 268-270
Boucher, Wayne, 63
Brookings Institute, 75
Brown v. the Board of Education, 90
Brown, Arnold, 60
Bibliographic Retrieval Service, 75, 134
Building Societies Association, 73
Bureau of Labor Statistics, 71
Business Roundtable, 12
Business Week, 74
BYTE, 74

Carson, Rachel, 86, 89
Chicago Tribune, 13, 72
Christian Science Monitor, The, 72
Civil Rights Act of 1964, 90
Clarkson, Max, 136
Clean Air Act, 89
Clean Water Act, 89
Clerical Workers Union, 95
Coalition for Office Technology, 95-96
Coates, Joseph, 61
Commerce, Department of, Bureau of Economic Analysis, 74
Computer World, 74
Congressional Quarterly, 75
Consensus report, 257-258
Consumer Product Safety Commission, 20, 92
Corvair, 92
Crossen, Cynthia, 83

Datamation, 74
dBase IV, 76
Delphi issue rating method, 123-128, 255-256
Development and Cooperation, 75
Dialogue, 75, 134
Digest of Public General Bills, The, 75
Digital Equipment Corporation (DEC), 39, 108, 146
Dingell, John, U.S. Representative, 14
Disability Act of 1992, 127, 195
Discover, 74
Dixon, W. MacNeile, 34, 214
Dow Corning Corporation, 13, 137

Eastman Kodak Company, 41, 71, 137
Ecodecision, 74
Economist, The, 81
Electro-magnetic fields, 71
Environment, 74
Environmental Protection Agency, 84
Equal Employment Opportunity Commission (EEOC), 92, 135
Equal Pay Act of 1963, 91, 92, 138
"Ergonomics," 94-96
Education Resource Information Center, 75

Fahey, Liam, 60, 62, 64, 65
Federal Register, 75
Federal Aviation Administration, 18, 93, 132
Feminine Mystique, The, 90
Financial Times, The, 74
Firestone Tire & Rubber, 15, 92, 137
Focus groups, 145
Food and Drug Administration (FDA), 12-13, 84, 96
Food industry, 7-8, 96
Food Lion, 205
Forbes, 74
Ford Motor Company, 8-9
Forst, Lisa, 274
Fortune, 74
Forum for Applied Research and Public Policy, The, 73
Friedan, Betty, 90
Friends of the Earth, 74
Future Survey Annual, 72
Futures, 73
FutureScan 2000, 72
Futurist, The, 73

Gates, Bill, 41
General Motors Corporation, 41
General Electric Company, 89, 92
Georgia-Power Company, 271-273
German Development Agency, 74-75
Global FutureScan 2000, 72
Global Network, The, 72
Global Tomorrow Coalition, 74
Guardian, The, 73

Harley-Davidson, 71
Harsard, 75
Health and Social Services, Department of, 73
Heath, Robert, 138
Heldres Publications, 74
Housing industry, 51-53
Hudson Institute, 75

In These Times, 75
Independent, The, 73
Industrial revolution, 41
"Infoductiveness," 99
Infant Formula Action Coalition (INFACT), 138
Information technology (IT), 114
Infoworld, 74
Institute for Crisis Management, 16, 17
Institute for the Future, 75
Insurance Institute for Highway Safety, 9
Interfaith Center for Corporate Responsibility (ICCR), 138

International Business Machines, 39, 41, 71, 108, 146, 213-214
Interstate commerce, regulation of, 264-268
Intolerable Risk: Pesticides in our Children's Food, 84
Island Press, 74
Issue abstract, 233-234
Issue accountability model, 149-154
Issue action plan, 143
Issue action team, 131-132
Issue analysis worksheet, 157-164
Issue briefs, 113-120, 192-193, 249-251
Issue categories, 123-124, 151-154, 193-194
Issue definition, 123, 133-134
Issue evaluation 126
Issue focus, 125
Issue identification, 192
Issue life cycle, 81-100
Issue maintenance, 152
Issue management process, 131-146
Issue monitoring, 153, 196-197
Issue owner, 127-128, 131, 151
Issue priority assignment, 126
Issue stage of development, 125
Issues vulnerability audit, 103-110, 245-246

John Naisbitt's Trend Letter, 72
Johnson, Lyndon, 90-91

Kessler, David, 12-13
King, 64
Kiplinger Washington Letter, 72
Kubler-Ross, 88

L.A. Department of Water and Power, 261-264
Lexis, 134
Linear thinking, 27-28
Lloyds Bank, 74
Los Angeles Times, 72

Machiavelli, Niccolo, 59, 201
Magaziner, Ira, 51
Manville Corporation, 137
McCarthy, Eugene, 89
McDonald's Corporation, 7-8, 20-21, 117, 205
Miami Herald, 72
Microsoft, 41
Mintzberg, Henry, 25, 35
Missawa Homes, Inc., 53
Molitor, Graham, 86
Money, Inc., 74
Money Programme, 74
Monthly Labor Review, The, 74
Morrison, James, 63
Mother Jones, 75
Ms, 73

Nader, Ralph, 92
Narayanan, 60, 62, 64, 65
Nation, The, 73
National Assn. of Manufacturers, 81
National Center for Health Statistics, The, 73
National Conference of State Legislatures, 75
National Cattlemen's Assn., 274-278
National Journal, The, 75
National Organization for Women, 95
National Review, The, 64, 75
National Technical and Information Services, 73
Natural Resources Defense Council, 84
Nature, 74
Nelson, Richard, 138
Nestlé Corporation, 138
Neufeld, William, 67
New Republic, The, 64, 75
New Scientist, 74

New Society, 73
New Statesman, 75
New York Times, The, 64, 72, 81
Newspaper Guild, The, 95
Newsweek, 73
Nexis, 134
Nolan, Joseph, 82

Occupational Safety & Health Administration, 71
Ogilvy, James, 45
Ohmae, Kenichi, 34
Olsen, Kenneth, 39, 108
O'Malley, Gary, 278
Oracle, 76
Organization for Economic and Cooperative Development (OECD), 73

Public Affairs Information Service, 75
Paradigms, 45-47
Pepsi, Diet, 117
Perot, Ross, 12
Personal Bibliographic Software, 75-76
Pesticides, 89
Peters, Tom, 25
Petroleum industry, 54-55, 229, 245-246
Pillsbury, 108
Political action committee (PAC), 144
Pro-Cite, 75
Pro-Search, 76
Proceedings of the National Academy of Sciences, 74
Professional Air Traffic Controllers Organization (PATCO), 6-7
Public Opinion, 73

Renfro, William, 63
Repetitive stress injuries, 70-72, 142
Royal Society of Canada, 74
Royal Dutch Shell, 19-20

Sambo's, 108
Sara Lee Corporation, 71, 142
Scanning, 63-64, 65-67
Scenario technique, 167-188
Schwartz, Peter, 45
Science, 74
Scientific American, 74
Sculley, John, 213
Sears, Roebuck and Company, 9-10, 38-39, 41, 70, 71, 92, 138, 237-239, 264-268
Seiko, 53-54
Senge, Peter, 9-10
Sierra Club, 74
Silent Spring, 86
Situational assessment, 133-134
60 Minutes, 205
SRI International, 103
Stakeholders, 136-140
Starling, Grover, 85
Steel industry, 50-51
Steering committee, 151, 153-154
Strategic thinking, 25-42
Strategic trend intelligence system, 59-78
Streep, Meryl, 84
Stress, 114

Taco Bell, 108
Tainted Truth, 83
Taxonomy, scanning, 69-70, 237-239
Taylor, Frederick, 25
Technological revolution, 41
Technological Review, 74
Telecommunications, 177-180
Teleconferencing, 115, 116, 118, 119
The Economist, 74
The Rise and Fall of Strategic Planning, 25
Three Mile Island, 33
Time, 73
Times, The, 73
Total Quality Management (TQM), 207-208
Tylenol, 117, 118, 119

U.S. News and World Report, 73
Uniroyal, 84

United Airlines, 18-19, 71, 93, 94-96, 146, 196, 204
United Kingdom Department of Trade and Industry, 73
United Nations, The, 73
United States
  Census Bureau, 73
  Department of Agriculture, 84, 96
  Department of Energy, 74
  Department of Labor, 73, 74
  Department of Transportation, 93, 132, 206
  Department of Treasury, 74
  League of Savings Associations, 73
Utné Reader, 73

Vaseff, James, 271
Video display terminals (VDTs), 71, 94-96, 146, 196, 204
Video text, 115
Vital Speeches of the Day, 73

Wall Street Journal, The, 64, 72
Washington Post, 72, 81
Weekly Report, 75
Weiner, Edith, 60
Weyerhaeuser Company, 278-282
Whistle blowing, 17
Whole Earth Review, The, 74
Wild-card events, 37
Wilson, Ian, 59, 88
Wood, Arthur, 92
Wood, General Robert E., 71
World Health Organization (WHO), 138
World Future Society, The, 72
World Monitor, 73
Worldwatch Institute, 74

Xerox Corporation, 41

About the Authors

William C. Ashley is founder and president of Ashley & Associates. He has twenty-five years of progressive and successful experience in leading market driven companies. He was chief architect of the Proactive Issues Management and Strategic Trends Systems at Sears, McDonalds and United Airlines. Mr. Ashley is an organizational psychologist by education and experience, a merchant by training and a leading proponent of proactive management techniques by design and dedication.

James L. Morrison received his Ph.D. at the Florida State University in 1969. He was lecturer in sociology at the University of Maryland, European Division and graduate assistant in sociology at the University of Munich (1964-65), instructor in sociology at the Florida State University (1968-69), and assistant professor of education and sociology at the Pennsylvania State University (1969-73). He moved to his current position at the University of North Carolina at Chapel Hill as associate professor of education in 1973 and was promoted to full professor in 1977. He teaches doctoral level courses in planning and evaluation.